Curious Cumbrian Walks

Curious Cumbrian Walks

Forty intriguing Lakeland rambles

Graham Dugdale

First published in 2011
by Palatine Books,
Carnegie House,
Chatsworth Road
Lancaster LA1 4SL
www.carnegiepublishing.com

Copyright © Graham Dugdale, 2011

British Library Cataloguing-in-Publication data
A catalogue record for this book is available from
the British Library

ISBN: 978 1 874181 73 6

Printed by Halstan Printing Group, Amersham, UK

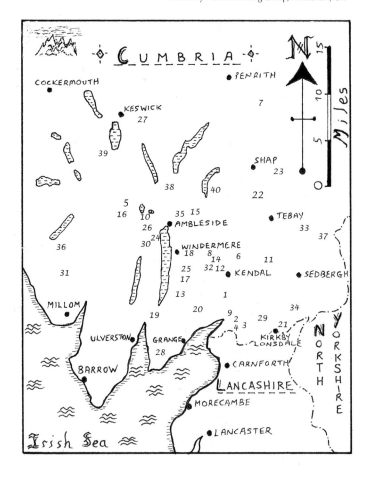

Contents

Introduction

'If it ain't broke, don't fix it!' A motoring adage that is equally applicable to the *Curious Walks* guide books. So successful was the format of *Curious Lancashire Walks* that to change it would indeed be needless tinkering. This volume therefore sticks closely to the original format, subject of course to a few minor tweaks and improvements suggested by the publisher.

As the title implies, these walks are all based in and around the delectable county of Cumbria. They are located both inside and outside the boundary of the Lake District National Park, and all have appeared in the *Lancaster Guardian,* for which I was the walks compiler during twelve happy years until my retirement in 2010.

Like a moth to a flame, I have always been constantly drawn back to Cumbria because of its upland terrain. The mountains are a stunning attraction that I for one find impossible to ignore. But as this volume shows, the county enjoys a wealth of scenic beauty far beyond the well-known honey pots centred on Keswick, Ambleside and Coniston.

My intention has always been to take readers into those areas that tend to be overlooked. Places that are not on the standard must-do list offered to tourists by well-meaning information centres. This guide invites you to do as the avid Trekky would do and 'boldly go where no man has gone before.' Well, maybe not quite. But you get the message.

With this in mind I could ask who has visited or even heard of the scintillating Lyvennet Valley? Or ventured over the fells to the east of Haweswater? Then there is Devoke Water in the west. A more remote yet enchanting tarn I have yet to behold.

There again, you might wish to marvel at the view that the celebrated walker Alfred Wainwright gazed upon from Orrest Head during his first Lakeland holiday. And even in the most popular valley of Great

Langdale, you can still find places to sit in isolation, quietly admiring Mother Nature's awesome handiwork.

Human curiosities also are to be found in profusion. In the company of your intrepid guide and his wife you will visit places likely to invoke gasps of wondrous pleasure when seen for the first time. Enjoy thwarting revenue men with Lanty Slee as he delivers yet another batch of his homemade moonshine (Walk 16). Shiver as the cold hand of Roger de Leyburne tickles your backbone on Cunswick Fell (Walk 12). Or you might wish to stroll in the spirited company of the Cistercian monks who lived at Cartmel Priory (Walk 28). But not on race day.

These and many other strange anomalies litter the dramatically fascinating Cumbrian landscape. My hope is that this guide, together with its companion Lancashire volume, will encourage readers to get out and about experiencing first hand the eccentric, the quaint or merely the unusual features that adorn their local area.

The Walks

All of the walks follow a circular route starting and finishing at the same place. They are thus designed primarily for those with access to a car. Indeed many of these walks are inaccessible to those who are forced to rely on public transport. They follow a ranking order that begins with the easiest, slowly building to more serious adventures.

The listing is arbitrary and my own personal view. Should you chance to agree, it will be a first and most definitely worthy of a pub lunch any day. Don't forget your cheque book.

Even though the last four walks will take you into traditional mountain country by visiting summits that exceed the magical two thousand feet, actual height of ascent remains below that figure.

There is something here for everybody to enjoy, along with the unusual, the strange and the downright quirky that can be visited along the way. And they should all be within the capabilities of, dare I say it, the averagely fit walker. The hand-drawn routes offer a good idea of the course to be followed but are not intended to replace the relevant Ordnance Survey map.

Warning

You are strongly urged to keep well away from cattle, especially after they have calved. These heavyweights will fiercely protect their young, and who can blame them. So always have an escape route figured out when crossing occupied fields. This advice is given from bitter personal experience following a near-fatal incident involving your intrepid guide.

Disclaimer

All these walks were correct at the time they were first undertaken. Some have been repeated and amendments duly made where necessary. The high fells never change. However, as the vast majority of these walks are at lower levels minor changes might be encountered, such as new fences, stiles or gates that can quickly appear and disappear. Rights-of-way will only change to avoid private land if the authorities give permission. Please take these provisos into consideration before setting out.

Acknowledgements

First and foremost I would like to thank my wife Ann for accompanying me on most of these walks; her constant good humour and encouragement were a tonic that made the whole project a delightful endeavour.

To readers of the *Lancaster Guardian* I owe a special debt of gratitude for their positive comments and suggestions that have made the 'Walk This Way' series such a success over the twelve years that it ran.

And finally a heartfelt thank you to Anna Goddard and all at Carnegie for their support and belief that made *Curious Lancashire Walks,* the companion volume to this offering, such a resounding success.

So if you're ready, it's best foot forward, happy hiking, and let's go!

Park at Levens
A glorious galaxy of ghosts, goats & gardens

DISTANCE:	4.5 miles (7.2 km)
HEIGHT:	450 feet (137 m)
START & FINISH:	Park in the lay-by on the old A6 just beyond the sharp left after crossing Levens Bridge.
GRID REFERENCE:	496853
TERRAIN:	Easy walking over rolling fields with a river cut limestone valley
NEAREST SHOPS:	Milnthorpe
USEFUL MAP:	OS Explorer OL7 English Lakes south east

Prelude

Grand, gorgeous and graceful! Here are some more great words to describe the extravaganza that is Levens, both Hall and Park. Few stately homes have more to offer the discerning walker in such a splendid setting. Located close to the last stage of the River Kent before it debouches into Morecambe Bay, Levens Hall lies some distance from the village that bears its name.

Dating back to 1188, the current main house was built towards the end of the first Elizabethan era. Topiary, which is the art of hedge and tree design, has brought international acclaim to the hall. The owners were most fortunate to have acquired the laudable expertise of landscape guru Monsieur Guillaume Beaumont, who began his long-term project of laying out the gardens from 1689.

Fashions come and go but the essential design as created by the French gardener has survived unchanged and includes many rare plants not found elsewhere. Stylishly pruned trees of beech, box and yew peep over the outer wall as you approach the well-known river crossing point at Levens Bridge.

A more romantic locale you would be hard pressed to find. But beware of numerous ghostly visitations that are known to inhabit the hall. Of these perhaps the occurrence known as the Luck of Levens *is the most intriguing. The legend is that whenever a white fawn is born to the herd of black fallow deer that roam the Park, momentous events will occur soon after.*

One gamekeeper was ordered to shoot such a creature to preserve the dark strain of the herd. He refused but the lord of the manor instructed another employee to carry out the grim action. It came as no surprise that an array of disasters befell the residents of Levens Hall soon after. This and many other strange tales can be enjoyed at Levens.

Any time spent visiting the impressively fortified house within its unique setting will most assuredly be worth the entrance fee. But let's enjoy the walk first.

The Walk

We begin by crossing the River Kent via Levens Bridge and taking a left through a small gate in the wall to enter the planned woodland of Levens Park. Hugging both sides of the river for a mile (1.6 km) up to the cataract of Park Head Falls, our route follows the right bank. With a gradual ascent away from the river, the path joins a long avenue of oaks, which forms the main focus of the park like a majestic guard of honour.

On the left in the valley bottom the River Kent can be seen flowing around a low bank of shingle known as Charley Island. Could it once have been a sanctuary for a certain Mister Tod, that crafty hunter who causes such controversy? Foxes are also referred to as Old Charley. As you process along the straight avenue, watch out for the famed Baggot goats and black fallow deer that roam Levens Park.

At the end of the avenue, bear right through another small gate to arrive at a back lane. Take a left towards Sedgwick over the main access road serving the motorway. Immediately on the far side, go

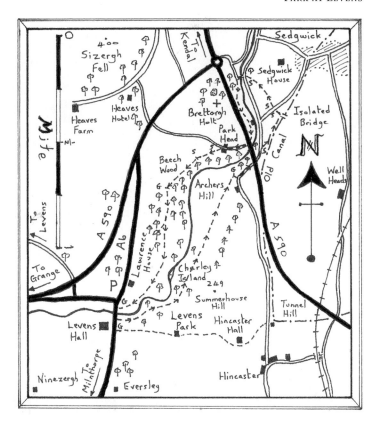

right up a flight of steps. A stile gives onto the course of the Lancaster Canal. Now abandoned and filled in, it is completely unrecognisable as such.

Follow a thin path which accompanies a fence towards the north west. The next bridge, cloaked in ivy, has become isolated in an ocean of grass. Rumours abound that the canal is to be re-excavated through to Kendal. But so far this has come to nothing due to the prohibitive expense.

Levens Hall oozes mystery and intrigue   A bridge too far!

Drop down to Sedgwick Lane below on the left where two old stiles give access to the path on the far side. Make a half-left crossing of the field with Sedgwick House over to your right. Another back lane is soon gained via another stile. Impressive iron railings suggest that this was once an entrance to the hall. Immediately opposite, a road bridge crosses the River Kent.

At this point the river presents a vigorous image, plunging between layers of eroded limestone scarring surrounded by a curtain of trees. An impressive sight to linger over before swinging left along a narrow lane that terminates just beyond some cottages. The path, however, winds beneath the motorway access road on a raised concrete platform above the river with vehicles thundering overhead.

Join the road at the far side, strolling onward for another 200 yards (183 m) to Park Head. Over to your right, ensconced in a sylvan cloak, is Brettagh Holt, a retreat for an order of nuns known as the Silesian Sisters. Mount a stile just beyond Park Head on the left to cross a field to the edge of Beech Wood. Hidden from view until the last minute, another stone ladder-stile is then crossed. Walk along the wall on your left up to a gated stile at the top end.

On the far side, drop down into the pastures of Levens Park now on the west side of the River Kent. Make your way around to the right above the valley floor, keeping the woods on your right as height is gradually lost on this smooth carpet of green turf. This pleasant stroll offers a satisfying end to a short walk that holds one's attention throughout. Join the main road near Levens Bridge turning left back to the lay-by.

At Holme in Beetham

An interesting transit between villages of contrasting heritages

DISTANCE:	5.5 miles (8.8 km)
HEIGHT:	150 feet (46 m)
START/FINISH:	Park at Beetham on the old section of road beside the bridge spanning the River Bela
GRID REFERENCE:	497796
TERRAIN:	A broad grassy depression sandwiched between limestone uplands
NEAREST SHOPS:	Beetham Post Office
USEFUL MAP:	OS Explorer 7 Lake District south east

Prelude

This walk traverses the mile-wide gap separating the Silverdale/Arnside Area of Outstanding Natural Beauty and the brooding upthrust of Farlton Fell. It provides an important link between north and south where every form of land transport is represented. Here lies a history lesson in communication on the ground which was occasioned by the retreat of the ice sheet south during the Ice Age some ten millennia past.

Numerous rights-of-way first appeared many centuries ago connecting isolated farms and villages. These are still made use of today by all walkers who love and enjoy the countryside. Some have been accorded specific titles depicting their importance to the modern rambler. Most famous in the north of England are the Pennine Way and the Coast-to-Coast. On this walk there is a small section connecting Beetham with Holme known as the Limestone Link. It is a medium-distance footpath from Arnside to Kirkby Lonsdale.

Small tracks and lanes gave way to water transport when the era of canals was born. The Lancaster Canal offered a steady, if slow, movement of bulky materials between Kendal and Preston, taking advantage of the relatively level nature of the terrain. The main west coast railway line is one of the most important in the country. More recent is the provision of the M6 motorway facilities for the general movement of goods and people.

As the land is low-lying and lacking an adequate natural drainage system, an extensive network of dykes has been excavated to allow surface water to escape. This means that arable crops have surrendered to the general pasturage of cattle and sheep. Some of the better drained areas are, however, still able to grow water-resistant crops such as swede and turnips.

Along with the major transport features, the villages in consequence are situated along the edge of the mossland above the flood plain. In the past they took advantage of springs that gushed from the limestone crevices on either side of the vale. Only the odd farmstead is encountered when crossing from one side of the mossland to the other.

Beetham received a mention in the Norman Domesday Book, being listed under the name of Biedun. It has been bypassed by the main road which once passed through its narrow main street. Today the village is dominated by the magnificent church of St Michael and Archangels. It dates from the twelfth century and was restored to full glory in the nineteenth century. This was when Saxon crosses from the reign of Edward the Confessor were found. Stained glass windows were severely damaged by Oliver Cromwell's forces in 1647.

Today it is a Grade One listed building constructed of limestone with a dressing of sandstone. A stone carving of the archangel Michael is located in a niche on the outside. One of the church's most notable features is the leafy tunnel leading from the back lane to the entrance doorway.

The church was at one time the nearest consecrated ground for burials to be conducted. Beetham lay at the eastern end of the Corpse Road, via which coffins were manhandled from Arnside and the west for burial in the graveyard. This difficult journey ended in 1866 when Arnside had its own church consecrated.

The Walk

From the old bridge spanning the River Bela, walk south along the main road until you reach the entrance to Beetham Hall. Cross over and take the wide track heading east across the gently rolling landscape of Holme Moss. Beyond the first farm buildings, lean right beside a small dyke. Go through a gate, then across a field locating a hedge stile. Thereafter lean half left to reach a back lane heading left past Beckside Farm.

After crossing Pye's Bridge, take the first gate on the right to mount a low hillock. Keep to the hedge on your left over the crest and down the far side. Enter the next field over a stile following a fence on the left to its far end where an offset double entry on the left allows passage over to the green footbridge spanning the railway.

This is the infamous field where your intrepid guide was 'aggressively' challenged by recalcitrant bovines protecting their young. A short crossing on the far side will bring you to a lane by way of another stile. Up on the right is Greystone. Built in 1875, it was home to the owner of Holme Mills. Go straight over, passing through four more stiles to

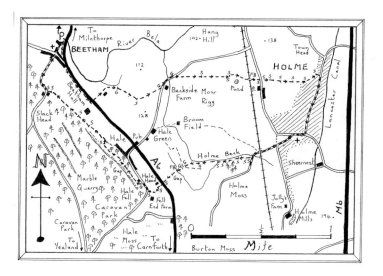

reach the new housing development on the edge of Holme. Keep to the left to enter a narrow ginnel that will bring you onto the main street.

Head right then right again at a T-junction to arrive at the village centre, comprising a post office and the Smithy Inn. Holy Trinity Church was built in 1839, catering to the spiritual needs of the expanding population. In the mid-nineteenth century, Holme was a booming village with a huge influx of young people working at the mills that lie half a mile to the south.

> *A self-sufficient community, the canal was specially routed to Holme to pass close to the mill. Completed in 1819, it enabled Holme to prosper. A mill has existed on the site since the thirteenth century for corn, flax and most recently carpets. One special product in the early days was the processing of jute, used in the manufacture sacking and, of course, carpets.*

Take the first lane forking left. When it swings sharply left towards Holme Mills, keep ahead to pass under the railway. After another 100 yards (91 m) the lane forks left. At this point, watch for a stile by a gate

Stroll down the rambling rose corridor to Beetham Church

Beetham Hall with its sturdy old pele tower

on the right immediately beyond a clear track. Count off seven stiles (the sixth hidden in some bushes on the right) as the path keeps close to Holme Beck.

When the beck veers away to the left, keep heading due west to reach a hedged track after a quarter mile (402 m) gated at each side. On the other side, continue onward, now in a south westerly direction. A dyke is negotiated by a foot bridge after which you should make your way up to the main road. Cross straight over, ambling up a track that serves Hale Head.

Bear right then left through a stile, keeping right of the building to enter a wooded area. The path bends to the right reaching a back lane by Fell End Farm. Head right for 164 yards (150 m) then fork left at a cottage to take the woodland path heading north west. Maintain a straight course, admiring the enchanting fairy grotto on your right.

On reaching a 'No Entry' sign, bear right then left to emerge through a wall-stile into an open field below the tree cover. Accompany the field path with Beetham Park on your left. A short distance after the next wall-stile, fork away half right to make a diagonal crossing of the grassland behind Beetham Hall.

The ancient pele tower, dating from the fourteenth century, now lies in ruins. It is one of many in the area including Arnside, Hazelslack and the best preserved of all at Sizergh Castle.

This one at Beetham was taken from the Royalists by Thomas Fairfax during the Civil War in 1644. A fortified manor house it was originally built to protect locals from marauding Scots sweeping down from the north. Stone walling surrounds the tower which rose to three storeys in height. The current farm-house was added in 1653.

Continue past the hall through two more stiles to reach Beetham village.

A short stroll past the elegant facade of the Wheatsheaf Hotel, built in the seventeenth century, completes an unusual and thoroughly stimulating walk encompassing a wide variety of scenery.

A Royal Welcome for the Mail

The village that time forgot

DISTANCE:	4 miles (6.4 km)
HEIGHT:	200 feet (61 m)
START/FINISH:	Parking in Burton is restricted to the side roads branching off the narrow main street. Tan Pits Lane is the best option
GRID REFERENCE:	528766
TERRAIN:	Rolling grassland pastures on limestone foothills plus the canal walk
NEAREST SHOPS:	Burton-in-Kendal
USEFUL MAP:	OS Explorer OL7 English Lakes south east

Prelude

Barely ten miles from Lancaster and just inside the Cumbrian boundary, Burton-in-Kendal has expanded into a commuter village for people who use the motorway to reach their place of employment. The old core, although surrounded by modern housing, still retains a rustic charm that few other settlements in the area can match.

Stroll up Tan Pits Lane, which dates back to 1750 when leather making was an important industry in the area. On the left just before Main Street is where the original pits were located. When first excavated, hair scraped from the raw leather was found here. Bear right along the narrow main street to imbibe the timeless appeal of a village that harkens back to the old coaching days.

Opposite the exotically named Neddy Hill can be found Cocking Yard. A narrow cobbled street of old cottages, it harkens back to a distant age when cock-fighting was a favoured pastime. To our right can be seen an unusual feature of the buildings on the main street. The first floor overhang that now offers shelter to pedestrians used to be where the village baker carried on his vital trade.

Those were nostalgic times, when the posthorn heralded the arrival of the mail coach, always a time of excitement for people who rarely ventured beyond the limits of their own villages. For in the early nineteenth century, Burton was on the principal north-south route, its grand hotels catering to the needs of tired travellers.

Then came the age of the canal and finally the railway. The station was built a mile to the north west around some cottages and an inn. This latter is still open for business. Along with many other village stations, Burton was axed during the infamous Beeching era of the early sixties.

Since the A6 and finally the motorway took the bulk of traffic away, Burton has returned to its tranquil heritage of yesteryear. The Kings Arms is still very much alive and catering to the needs of twenty-first century travellers, unlike the Royal Hotel in the village square which has been forced to close its doors. I am reliably informed that it will not be opening for business of a similar nature in the foreseeable future.

Take a peep behind the King's Arms where the original stable block has hardly altered, and view the remains of the ancient market cross where corn was traded. Only a stone column remains today, unlike when the monks stood upon this spot to preach before a permanent church was built. Fixtures on the base do, however, indicate where leg irons of felons were secured, proving that all was not sweetness and light in the Burton of our forebears.

The Walk

Our circular tour begins by strolling up a constricted passage at the side of the Royal Hotel adjoining the 'cross'. Walk up the hedged corridor until it bends left at the top end of a large field. Heading north, the path wanders behind modern housing to reach a back lane. Cross straight over along this narrow track, hedged throughout.

An ancient right-of-way called Slape Lane, it pursues a north-westerly course across the slopes below Hutton Roof Crags. Just beyond a narrow wood, we arrive at a gate bearing left between stands of trees.

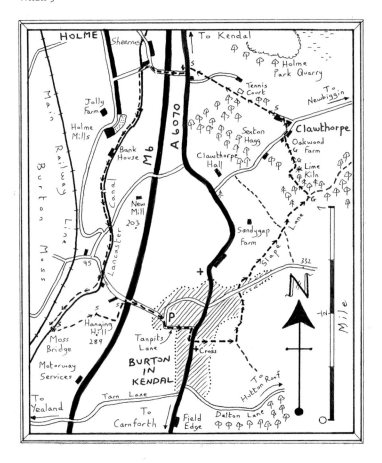

The track veers right at a wall before continuing onward past a large old lime kiln and through a gate.

After passing through another gate, keep to the right of Oakwood Farm across a metalled concourse, thus gaining the fell road through a wall-gap. Lean right then left up the access lane serving the tiny hamlet of Clawthorpe.

Another left at a T-junction will bring you to a gate where a splendidly stepped limestone stile is mounted. In the open parkland beyond, take a direct course down the middle of the field, with loose stands of woodland on either side. Clawthorpe Hall can, be seen through the trees on your right.

After passing to the left of a tennis court, a metalled access road is crossed. Keep straight ahead, aiming right of the estate lodge to straddle a stile giving onto the A6070 Burton road. Head left then immediately right to cross over the motorway where you need to head left again along a narrow lane serving a canalside row of terraced cottages known as Sheernest. After crossing the Lancaster Canal, join the towpath to head south.

Accompany this once important waterway for about 1.5 miles (2.4 km) until you reach the second bridge. On this section, the canal passes over two roads. Watch out for a canal information plaque that offers a fascinating insight into the history of this unique historical feature.

Saunter over Moss Bridge, aiming half left up to a hedge where a stile is crossed. Straddle the crest of Hanging Hill, speculating whether this was where baddies were cordially invited to attend their very own necktie party. Then amble down the far side with a hedge on your right. At the bottom, bear left to reach a lane, then right over the motorway and back into Burton.

Burton's market cross holds centre stage | Unusual overhanging second storeys

Linger Amidst the Limestone

Walker's paradise in an abandoned quarry

DISTANCE:	6.5 miles (10.5 km)
HEIGHT:	100 feet (30 m)
START/FINISH:	Roadside parking just past the Leighton Moss access track a quarter mile NE of the RSPB visitor centre
GRID REFERENCE:	480753
TERRAIN:	Extensive woodland with underlying limestone bedrock where numerous open scar crags are in evidence
NEAREST SHOPS:	Silverdale
USEFUL MAP:	OS Explorer OL7 English Lakes south east

Prelude

Although much of this walk lies within the Lancashire boundary, its northern extremity does wander across into Cumbria, so justifying its inclusion in this volume. It is quite a simple expedition but it does require careful negotiation due in part to the large amount of woodland and irregular stone walls. This can make orientation somewhat difficult with identifiable landmarks in short supply.

However, if the limestone type of scenery catches your fancy, this walk is an ideal jaunt to enjoy up close and personal. Scarring identified by horizontal slabs of exposed layering of rock is an enjoyably distinctive feature of the early stages.

We are so close to the Leighton Moss bird sanctuary that it would be a great pity not to visit the centre just down the road. Close to where we park, a track heads across the moss towards Leighton Hall. In the middle of this is a public viewing hide from which all manner of feathered visitors can be welcomed. Even the rare bittern is known to favour Leighton Moss so listen out for its distinctive mooing chorus.

If you have time, pay a visit to the splendid RSPB visitor centre, but not before you have enjoyed the splendid walk on offer.

The Walk

Begin by strolling up the road to pass through the gate giving access to the golf course. Continue straight ahead along the edge of a characteristic wedge of limestone scarring on your right. After a short distance a unique metal gate is reached, installed to the memory of a local walker called John Mabson. Take the time to ponder over the poignant ode etched onto a plaque.

Just beyond, circle around a tumble of dislodged rocks, thereafter bearing right into the open trough of Trowbarrow Quarry.

This an elongated dish in the underlying rock which was first quarried in 1857 to take advantage of the new railway. Prior to this, it was not commercially viable.

The quarry prospered, employing hundreds of men who dug the rock out using simple hand tools. Gas works, tanneries and paper mills were the principle customers along with cement works, not forgetting the use of limestone as a fertiliser. Also worth noting is that Trowbarrow was where road macadam was first manufactured.

The quarry finally shut down in 1959 and is today a favourite haunt of rock climbers. Excellent routes have been established on the main rock face although recent falls have rendered some of the climbs out of bounds.

Bear left down the main quarry access track, at the start of which can be seen the foundations of the Tallyman's Hut where each quarry worker had to record his daily output.

Stroll down the track, passing through two gates at the bottom and bearing right up the road serving Hawes Water. After passing a row of cottages, lean right through a gate continuing along the wall before

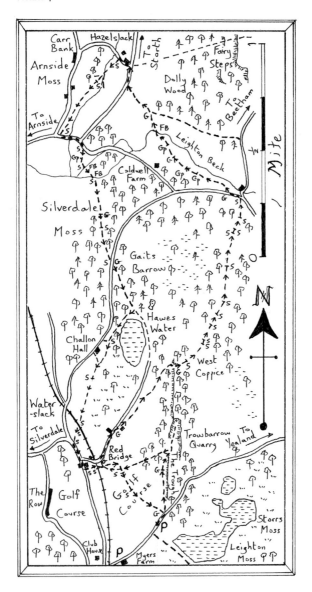

Ann reads about Trowbarrow
Nature Reserve

Trowbarrow holds an attraction for
rock climbers

leaning away to enter the woods on a gentle climb. Keep heading north east to reach a wall-gate. The path soon slants to the right along another wall where a stile brings you into an open field.

Keep with this wall across to a stile on the far side. Wander through thick undergrowth on a clear path. Beyond a stile at the far side, enter another open stretch with a stile after 100 yards (91 m) where deer can often be seen prancing about. Follow the thin yet obvious path in the grass around to a fence-stile. Take the left of two paths along the edge of the woods on your left. Keep heading due north over five stiles to reach Leighton Beck Bridge.

Bear left for 100 yards (91 m) then slant right through a gate. Accompany the clear field track up to a foot bridge spanning Leighton Beck. Across the field is a gate giving access to a rough hedged lane. Stick with this to merge with the road close to Hazelslack Farm.

At the farm bear left, squeezing through a stile opposite another close to the farm's ancient pele tower, which was used for protection against brigands sweeping down from the north back in the fourteenth century. Leave the clear track when it closes with a caravan site on the right and make for the top left corner of the field. Go through a stile and accompany a path through the shrubbery. Be aware that this becomes a muddy quagmire following heavy rain.

After only a quarter mile, dry land is reached. Bear left along the road for 250 yards (229m), angling through the gate on your right. Now head south to a small copse, passing down a short walled corridor and arcing left to a fence-stile and slabbed footbridge.

Make a short crossing of the field to another. Walk alongside the wall on your right until a gate is reached. Beyond this a stile must be strad-dled then it is a short walk through the woods to reach the road. Go straight over into the nature reserve of Gait Barrows. A clear woodland trail will bring you to the reedy expanse of Hawes Water.

Char are known to inhabit Hawes Water

Approaching the fringe of this enchanted pool, keep a wary eye open for strange creatures skulking amidst the reed scarf that surrounds the silver sheen. Largest of the four tarns in the area, Hawes Water is renowned for its char, a fish of the trout family that abide therein. One can only wonder whether this Lakeland delicacy has helped to sustain a more sinister resident of the mere.

> In days of yore when the 'Dragon of Hawes Water' disturbed the peaceful tarn, churning it into a potent ferment, local people could expect trouble and discord to invade their humble community. This vile beast was likened to a worm and was said to have been cast into the tarn by a certain Roger de Conyers as a reminder of his dragon-slaying prowess.
>
> In the county of Durham, this brave knight had exterminated many dragons which terrorised the villages and preyed upon children and young maidens who strayed to close to their dens. Roger eventually married the daughter of landowner William de Lancaster and is thought to have cast at least one baby worm into the tarn which grew to full size.
>
> One can but speculate as to the origins of the story concerning the Hawes Water Dragon. Perhaps it was initiated by a poacher seeking to scare off those who sought to prevent his illicit purloining of the tasty char.

Take the path on the right of the tarn until a wall-stile on the left is reached. This is a recent alternative route that allows the building of Challon Hall to be bypassed.

Join the original path at the far side, continuing along the fenced off extremity of Hawes Water Moss. Beyond a fence-stile, care is needed when crossing the mainline railway. Join the road heading left. Immediately beyond Red Bridge Farm, bear left down a grass bank to re-cross the railway. A thin path enters the woods, soon crossing the Trowbarrow Quarry track.

A narrow path snakes up through the trees crossing back higher up to enter the hallowed links of Silverdale Golf Club. Watch out for flying golf balls as you cross to a wall-stile on the far side. Maintain a south-easterly bearing for the return to the gate near Leighton Moss.

The Short and the Long of it
A fine introduction to one of England's most popular valleys

DISTANCE:	4.5 miles (7.2 km)
HEIGHT:	200 feet (61 m)
START/FINISH:	200 yards (183 m) beyond Harry Place in Great Langdale, watch for a pull-in on the left
GRID REFERENCE:	311063
TERRAIN:	Classic glaciated scenery of the highest quality, Great Langdale has something to suit every taste
NEAREST SHOPS:	Chapel Stile
USEFUL MAP:	OS Explorer OL6 English Lakes south west

Prelude

My original intention for this particular day had been governed by the reliable predictions of the meteorological office. Their finely honed assertion was that the moorland country to the north east of Tebay would be clear and sunny. Lakeland was supposed to be cloudy and wet. Why do I always fall for it? Millions of pounds spent on the latest digital technology should allow them to get it right.

But no. Yet again they had let me down. How many times is that this year? A dense grey pall hung suspended over even the lowest fells. And peering over to the west, Lakeland shimmered in bright sunshine. A detour was clearly suggesting itself. Even the most optimistic fell-wanderer would have been hard pressed not to reverse and head over towards Kendal.

By the time we reached Great Langdale, I judged it to be too late in the day to attempt anything of a significant height. But this valley lends itself admirably to one of the finest valley walks in the District. With good paths all the way, as you would expect in such a popular locale, this is a walk that anybody can enjoy and in any weather, as was amply proven on this day.

Great Langdale has to be the most visited of all the valleys in Lakeland. Being so close to Ambleside and Coniston, it is so easy to reach. And the farther down valley one drives, the more exciting is the prospect on offer. Once Chapel Stile has been left behind, the upper valley opens up to reveal a truly mouth-watering spectacle of mountain treats.

Names such as Bow Fell, Crickle Crags, Harrison Stickle and Pike O'Blisco trip off the tongue as they jostle each other for centre stage. On this walk, we may not be setting foot on their knobbly summits, but we can still admire their scalloped profiles and make plans for another visit in the not-too-distant future.

The Walk

We begin by walking back up the road for 100 yards (91 m) to take the footpath crossing to the far side of the valley. It begins down a narrow rough-walled lane. Go through a stile keeping a straight course over another one and a small footbridge before leaning right towards a more substantial specimen spanning Great Langdale Beck.

The flat valley floor provides excellent pasture for both sheep and cattle. It is thought that this particular sector of the valley once contained a lake. Over time, material washed down by the many streams flowing off the fellsides has filled it in. This is not surprising in view of the fact that the valley has one of the highest rainfall levels in the country. When it rains in Great Langdale you know about it.

Sheep in profusion mingle with cattle grazing on the flat pastures surrounded by dry-stone walls. The first people to arrive in the valley were axe-makers from the Neolithic Stone Age period some 6000 years ago. A primitive factory has been unearthed on the higher slopes of Pike O'Stickle. More permanent occupation did not occur until the arrival of the Norse settlers in the tenth century.

The Celia Johnson pose on Middlefell Bridge

After crossing the bridge, bear right to circle round behind the isolated cottage of Oak Howe, taking the stony trail to head up valley. This path skirts the lower slopes of Lingmoor Fell which rises steeply on the left. Once you have passed through a stile, the path bends to the left to reveal the majestic splendour of the valley head.

On the far side, the distinctive shape of the Langdale Pikes is clearly visible. You can even make out the renovated footpath snaking up beside Stickle Ghyll. Like many other popular areas, millions of boots have caused severe erosion which will require drastic remedies if the fells are to retain their essential character.

A gate is soon reached which adjoins a sheepfold. Thereafter one of these newly laid paths drops down to Side House where a track connects with the valley road. Ignore the footbridge, climbing a short grass bank to mount a ladder-stile. Accompany a path in the grass through another wall-stile until a broken wall is reached.

Leave the path here to slant down to the trees below, where a stile giving access to the camp site is clearly in view. Pass through the trees

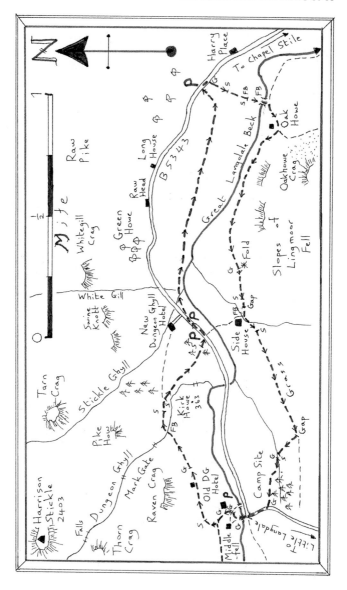

and over a footbridge to enter the site. Keep heading up valley to emerge through a gate onto the road coming down from Blea Tarn. Lean right down to a sharp bend where the B road officially starts.

Continue straight over up a rough track that crosses Great Langdale Beck by means of that stone bridge made famous in the film Brief Encounter. Here it was that the two illicit lovers dallied for a while. This being my wife Ann's favourite movie, a pause for the obligatory photocall was made.

Through the gate on the far side, swing right to cross the access road serving Middlefell Farm. On your right is the pub affectionately known as the Old DG.

> Originally a farm, it became the Middlefell Inn in 1885. Its current name of the Old Dungeon Ghyll was acquired when the new version was later built half a mile (800m) up valley.

> The Old DG has long been renowned in climbing circles and was given to the National Trust in 1928 by Professor G.M. Trevelyan. This was the first property that the Trust acquired in Langdale. It continued as a farm and hotel until 1949 when the shippon was converted into the Climbers' Bar.

> This well-known locale became a mecca for young climbers sharpening their claws on the local crags. Such luminaries as Chris Bonington, Don Whillans and Joe Brown were regular visitors. At that time, many of the climbing fraternity bedded down at Wall End Barn close to the Blea Tarn road. I have been reliably informed that many celebrations were enjoyed here that involved much quaffing of the amber nectar.

And so back to the walk. A narrow enclosed passage directs walkers to the valley track behind. Pass through the gate at the end to strike up the steepening fellside. Locate a stile and join the main track that continues up the valley into Mickleden. Our route heads back towards Chapel Stile.

But first take note of the rising pillar of rock looming above. This is Middlefell Buttress and has long been a handy crag for climbers to get in some practice before venturing uphill to the more awesome challenge of Gimmer Crag. Follow the track until you reach the stile just after the footbridge spanning Dungeon Ghyll itself.

Immediately following this one, go through another on the right to drop down through the bracken to reach the valley car park. Bear left along the road, forking right to accompany the old valley road. This particular track was superseded by the present motor road because of flood problems. It is quite a stony track, a feature that also applies to the bed of the beck. This is the material that was washed down from the heights above and helped fill in the valley floor.

The track bends to the left as the new road is neared, returning us to the start. This is a splendid introduction to the celebrated Langdale Valley that is mostly bypassed by the crowds. Nevertheless, you are still recommended to avoid bank holidays and weekends to obtain the most enjoyment.

A motor road has replaced this old highway

A quiet time to reflect in Great Langdale

A Minty Treat in the Foothills

Solitary rambling amidst unspoilt country remote from the beaten track

DISTANCE:	5.5 miles (8.6 km)
HEIGHT CLIMBED:	200 feet (61 m)
START/FINISH:	Four miles (6.4 km) north of Kendal on the A6 pull off at Otter Bank and park on a section of the old road
GRID REFERENCE:	532973
TERRAIN:	Rolling foothills that rise gradually towards the impressive Whinfell Ridge
NEAREST SHOPS:	Kendal
USEFUL MAP:	OS Explorer OL7 English Lakes south east

Prelude

It is unlikely that this walk will be included in the itinerary of any other like-minded groups or individuals. Not a soul was encountered throughout, which is just the way Ann and myself prefer it. The stretch of undulating country that lies just outside Lakeland's south-east border to the north of Kendal is barely afforded a glance by passing motorists.

Sandwiched between two main roads and the Whinfell Ridge, none of the numerous low hills reach anywhere near the 1000-foot contour. A dense network of dry-stone walls and fences criss-cross the area, interspersed with small isolated farms. Sidling between the irregular hillocks is the River Mint, eventually merging with the Kent at the northern edge of Kendal.

The Mint has often been referred to as the noisy river. The name is not derived from the wild variety growing on the banks. It comes from Mimmet which surfaced in the twelfth century and relates to bleating.

No doubt this refers to the large population of woollies that inhabit the fields hereabouts.

Footpaths are quite easy to follow, with the latter part of the ramble following the celebrated Dales Way. This is a long-distance footpath stretching 81 miles (130 km) from Ilkley to Bowness. You are recommended to try it sometime, allowing a week from end to end.

The Walk

Set off on this walk by heading north up the steep section of lane for 200 yards (183 m) until it veers right. At this point continue ahead along a wall/hedged rough track called Dry Lane. Although partly metalled, it is very narrow with much of the underlay having disintegrated. These days it is only used by farm vehicles. The large building seen over to the left is a water treatment plant. On reaching another lane, go through the gate off-set to the left. After this, Dry Lane goes onward as a wide grassy trod.

An impish sprite is said to haunt Selside Hall

Pause for a minute along this track to cast your eye over the fields towards the north west where Selside Hall can be seen. The farm is of fourteenth century origin, a solid edifice specially built for defence. In the days before electricity, a vexatious sprite used to rush about the house extinguishing all the candles and oil lamps. In the grounds stands an old yew tree where sheep stealers were hanged. One has to consider whether the spirit of one of these felons was seeking revenge on the occupants.

Pass through a wall-gate followed by another a quarter mile (402 m) ahead just before Light Water is crossed. This rather insignificant beck is one of the few watercourses named on the map, an honour that is testament to its stature in this area of few such distinctions. Beyond the gate just across from Light Water we pass right of Selside Endowed CE School. Erected in 1831 to serve the local farmers, it was expanded

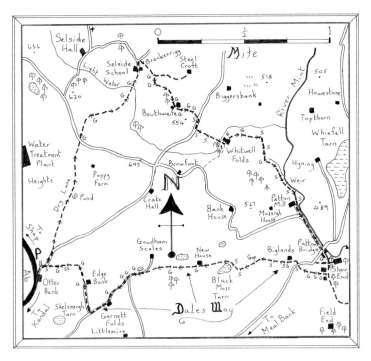

Some noisy residents join Ann near the Mint

in 1897 and is now a vital source of learning for the rural community hereabouts.

Stroll up the access road past Brackenrigg, turning sharp right along a fenced track which serves Steel Croft. At the first bend, lean right through a gate to cross a field to another gate. A clear track rises left on the far side leading down to Bouthwaite. Beyond the farm keep left, passing through a trio of gates with a wall on your right. The last one brings you into the field on the opposite side.

Drop down to reach a lane over a stepped wall-stile. Keep right for 100 yards (91 m), then it's left across the fields to a wood where we cross Light Water for the second time by a footbridge. Bear left between the buildings of Whitwell Folds down a narrow passage to enter a field.

On the day I passed this way, a bull was in residence. Should you meet up with a similar guardian, give him a wide berth by keeping to this side of the field. At the far side, pass through a gate, walking down to a stile. At the same time, keep a wary eye on the big guy should he be in residence.

Over the stile and we bear right, mounting a low rise along to the next wall-stile, thereafter dropping down to a depression. Go through the gate, heading left with a hedge and small stream on your left. This soon merges with the River Mint. Follow the right bank of the Mint all the way down to Patton Mill, noting the weir and its channelled diversion. This was originally used to power the mill although no evidence of such now remains.

Stroll down the access road to a T-junction. Continue ahead up a track offset on the right past Patton Cottages. After passing beneath the access road serving Shaw End we join the Dales Way to head right through a gate to pass a renovated barn.

The endowed school at Selside opened in 1831

The route follows a narrow corridor to emerge onto a lane opposite the entrance to Biglands. Go through the grounds to join a broad passage between a wall and hedge. After the second stile, this bends to the left up to a dead end where a wall-gap is crossed. Aim for a wall-stile to circle right round Black Moss Tarn.

Mount a low grass hill to reach New House on the far side. Keep left of the house to locate a gate and the start of a straight groove that eventually deposits you on the paved access road serving Goodham Scales. Pass through a trio of gates, forging ahead when the road veers left.

Drop down this paved track to pass through another gate just before Garnett Folds. Watch for a right turn which is where we leave the Dales Way. This access road will take you up to Edge Bank. Keep left of the farm buildings through a gate to cross the field behind.

Locate an iron gate in the hedge to pass around a low hill where an unusual double stile is negotiated. Keep alongside the wall on your left for the return to Otter Bank.

An Infamous Royal Connection

A village with a sinister past that knows how to enjoy itself

DISTANCE:	5 miles (8 km)
HEIGHT:	200 feet (61 m)
START/FINISH:	Beyond Orton on the B6260, take the third left for 3 miles (4.8 km) to reach King's Meaburn. Park on the grass verge at the start of the village
GRID REFERENCE:	623208
TERRAIN:	Rolling pastures sloping down to the main valley of the River Eden conceal the enclosed Lyvennet Ravine
NEAREST SHOPS:	Bolton (Eden Valley)
USEFUL MAP:	OS Explorer OL19 The Howgill Fells & Upper Eden

Prelude

The Eden Valley, lying between the Pennines and Lakeland fells, offers a major link between east and west by way of the A66. Yet surprisingly few visitors bother to take advantage of its charms. Apart from the towns of Appleby, Penrith and Carlisle, the valley is relatively unknown. And the tributary valley of the River Lyvennet is a hidden gem just waiting to be discovered.

Perhaps I shouldn't be heralding its attractions but ought instead to keep this delightful spot all to myself. But such is the generosity of your esteemed guide that he feels duty-bound to spread the good tidings to all who value peace and quiet. One occasion when things liven up considerably, though, is during the well-known annual beer festival held at the White Horse pub.

Villages such as Crosby Ravensworth, Maulds Meaburn and its cousin King's Meaburn stretch along the valley road. Myths and legends abound in Old Westmorland, many of which can be taken with a pinch of salt. The story attached to King's Meaburn, however, is firmly cemented in historical fact. For on the 29 December in the year 1170, the Lord of the Manor, Hugh de Morville, was involved in one of the most heinous events chronicled in medieval times.

The village of King's Meaburn dates from Anglo-Saxon times in the seventh and eighth centuries and means 'meadow by a stream'. Its royal connections have a far more sinister history. Hugh de Morville was implicated in the dastardly slaying of the Archbishop of Canterbury, Thomas Becket.

The monarch of the day Henry II became so incensed with the archbishop's entrenched attitude that he famously called for anyone to rid him of this thorn in his side. Four knights took the king at his word and promptly went to Canterbury, killing Becket on the altar of the cathedral. De Morville is said to have held the crowds at bay while the dirty deed was accomplished.

He was duly hanged for his crime when Henry denied all knowledge of the supposed request. All his lands were confiscated by the crown, half being granted to De Morville's sister, the lovely Maud. The incident has become a part of English history yet few people are aware of the part played by the village's infamous lord. The only other claim to historical fame occurred in 1745 when Bonny Prince Charlie crossed the river nearby with soldiers en route to a rendezvous at Shap.

The Walk

Our walk begins with a stroll up the hedged route that runs beside the old school house. Heading north east, the field track drops down into a shallow depression occupied by the narrow Coat Syke. An extensive caravan site is located on the right. At the end of this corridor, go through a gate followed immediately by another on the left.

Aim half right to the far side of the field, walking along the side of the hedge to a gate at the end. In the next field, keep outside the line of trees on the right passing through some others at the top end emerging into the on-going field over a stile.

Keep ahead through a gate followed by another stile. The path now changes to the left side of the hedge for 100 yards (91m). Make a diagonal crossing of two narrow fields with stiles at the midpoint of each. After this, drop down to cross Luz Beck by a stone slab. Climb out the far side along an enclosed passage to reach the main street of Bolton.

Bolton is a linear village stretching along the Appleby road. It grew to prominence at one of the few crossing points of the River Eden. A water-powered mill on the south bank of the river provided employment, although it is likely that the Roman encampment on the far side was the original reason for people settling here on a permanent basis.

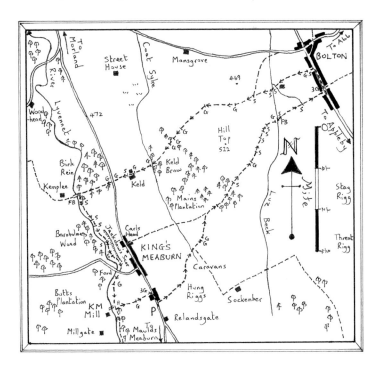

The thrashing rapids in the Lyvennet gorge

Heading left down the main highway of Bolton for 300 yards (274 m), watch for the signpost pointing west for the return to the Lyvennet. Mount a stile and gate to emerge into a long field behind the village street. Head straight down to straddle a hedge stile at the bottom where Luz Beck needs to be re-crossed. No handy footbridge this time.

Locate a stile on the far side then walk up beside a hedge to join a major track. Keep heading west to the end of the hedged corridor. Then take the right of two gates, following the fence on your left round to the next gate. Keep the fence on your left passing through a narrow wooded tract gated at each side.

Another 200 yards (183 m) and we enter another section of woodland likewise gated at each side. Cross the bridge spanning Coat Syke to approach the extensive farmstead of Keld. Pass through a wall-gap at the far side veering right to join the access track up to the main valley road.

Cross straight over for the walk down to the banks of the River Lyvennet itself. Bear left for the walk alongside this most beautiful of watercourses. Steep sandstone crags rear up on the left side as the river splutters and bubbles over a series of rapids. This idyllic section of river is completely hidden away.

Beyond Jackdaw Crag, the road crosses the river by means of a ford. We continue on the far side until King's Meaburn Mill is reached. It still has a large water-wheel and three circular stones that once used to grind the corn. The original applewood cogs and gearing are still in evidence.

Cross a stile on the far side of the access track. After only 20 yards (18 m) leave the path to climb up a rough banking to straddle a new fence at the top. No stile had been provided on my most recent visit, an oversight that I trust will soon be rectified.

With a newly planted and fenced hedge on the left, head for the far side of the field to pass through a gate. Ascend the facing slope, negotiating three more gates to reach the main street of King's Meaburn. A short amble to the right will return you to the start.

It is perhaps worth noting that the Eden Valley, unlike any other place in the country, can claim to possess its very own wind

The old corn mill still retains its water wheel

system. Known as the Helm Wind, it focuses on Cross Fell. You will be made well aware of its approach by the rampant chorus like t'blast from a bugle that cuts a ferocious sweep down through the gullies howling with the tormented agony of a thousand hounds from hell. The chain of villages lying directly in the path inevitably bear the remorseless brunt of its fury.

Girding up around Brampton to the north, the Helm can last for three or four days leaving a trail of chaotic destruction in its wake, and two weeks of unrepentant buffeting is not unusual. Springtime is the season for battening down the hatches in preparation for the coming onslaught. Such potent vigor is known to have blown sheep around like a scrap of paper, and once it was even rumoured that a horse and cart had been overturned, never to be seen again.

So in the finest scouting tradition, one should always 'be prepared'. Locals know that

> *When t'Helm's low, and foxes bark,*
> *Bar up your door afore its dark.*

King's Meaburn Endowed School is now a private residence

Norse Things Around Ings

Put out to grass by the Viking settlers

DISTANCE:	3.5 miles (5.6 km)
HEIGHT CLIMBED:	350 feet (107 m)
START/FINISH:	Pull off the main road at Ings and park on the side road keeping well into the side
GRID REFERENCE:	445987
TERRAIN:	A wild tangle of hillocks and shallow depressions cloaked in a dense network of stone walls
NEAREST SHOPS:	Staveley, or Ings Garage
USEFUL MAP:	OS Explorer OL7 English Lakes south east

Prelude

Bowling down the main road towards Windermere, the first rocky outcrop to be encountered is Reston Scar. It stands guard over the now bypassed village of Staveley and has given its name to the house immediately below. A handsome Georgian mansion half a mile (800 m) before Ings, this particular residence was built for Robert Bateman, who made his fortune in the sale of Italian marble. In 1743 he set off for home having been informed that his new house was ready for occupation.

Unfortunately he never arrived. Rumours abound as to his fate. It has been suggested that he was killed by the captain of his ship who then threw his body into the sea off Gibraltar. Robert's body may never have reached Ings, but his spirit certainly did. A ghost has frequently been seen hanging around the gates of the property and watching the house, although it has so far never ventured inside.

The intimation was that Bateman disliked women, which is why the fairer sex have not often lived in the house for very long. Ings Church was where the last consignment of marble was heading when Bateman disappeared. But did it ever arrive?

The village itself has been bypassed by the main road and receives few visitors except for those calling in at the more recent additions of the garage and cafe. Ings grew up around its mill which has now been converted into the splendid Watermill Inn. St Anne's Church nearby is a substantial edifice which implies that the village was an important focal point for the local farming settlements in the vicinity.

Robert Bateman provided funds to build the row of cottages on the opposite side of the road, which at the time were almhouses for the less fortunate members of the community. He clearly had a charitable nature, being also the benefactor of the local school. This is commemorated in a poem written about this local hero by William Wordsworth who was impressed with Bateman's endeavours. It relates how villagers raised a collection to send him to London whilst a young man, with the aim of securing a prosperous future.

The Walk

It is suggested that the rather short walk on offer here is best reserved for an inclement afternoon when the higher or longer walks have been abandoned. So start off by crossing the main road to stroll up a back lane that climbs gradually for half a mile (800 m) to reach the isolated hamlet of Grassgarth.

Dating back to the tenth century, it started as a small farming settlement operating on the strict Norse principle of allocated pasture to prevent over-grazing: one grass being equal to eight acres which was considered sufficient for a family to run. Animals grazed on the lower well-watered meadow around Ings in winter before transferring to the out-fields in summer, a process known as transhumance.

At Grassgarth the road becomes a rough track which forms the high level route into upper Kentmere. This gently shelving terrain is

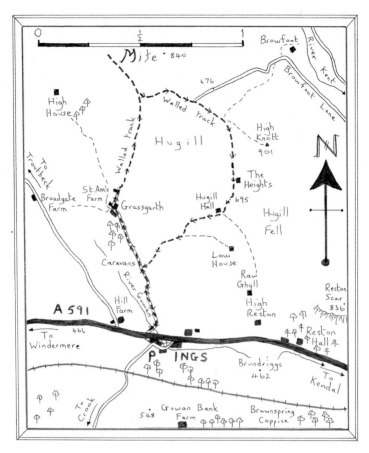

criss-crossed by an extensive network of dry-stone walls, making the surrounding tops difficult to visit. Make your way north until the walled track merges with another one.

Less than half a mile (800 m) further on are the remains of an early British settlement. It is located on private land, so a visit should be made with this proviso in mind.

Known as Hugill Village, it is one of numerous hut villages that were sited on higher land to avoid the badly drained pasture in the valley bottoms.

The buildings have not survived but the outlines can still be discerned by those with an active imagination.

Should you not wish to see the village, head sharp right soon passing the end of the paved road that comes up from Kentmere. A few hundred yards beyond this junction a prominent cairn can be seen to the left.

Note the stone plaque above the door of St Anne's Church

This is High Knott, better known locally as Williamson's Memorial. The splendidly proportioned cairn incorporates a tablet bearing the following inscription: 'In Memory of Thomas Williamson of Height in Hugill, Gent, who died Feb. 13th 1797. Aged 66 years. Erected 1803.'

Grassgarth was a Norse farming settlement

Reston House where Robert Bateman lived

Heights is the next settlement that we come to. It is now in disrepair and the memorial was erected by the Reverend Thomas Williamson for his father who used to climb to the summit of High Knott every morning before breakfast. Beyond Heights, the path becomes metalled for a short distance continuing south to Low House.

Our route bears right becoming rough again to pass Hugill Hall. This old farm has given its name to the surrounding locality, which is largely unknown to walkers. The path narrows beyond the hall as it drops down to merge with another path coming in from the left. After half a mile (800 m) we rejoin the Grassgarth's road heading left back down to Ings.

A rewarding finale would be to sample the delights afforded by the Watermill Inn. A truly excellent meal can be supplemented by one or more of the many guest beers on offer. Boasting an international complement as well as the host of real ales from this country, the choice is amazing. And by ensuring that your driver remains teetotal, the real ale aficionado can indulge himself with a clear conscience.

For those with canine companions, this pub is most assuredly a dog-friendly establishment.

A Deer Walk with Herons

Step lively or the fairies will grab you!

DISTANCE:	3.5 miles (5.6 km)
HEIGHT:	350 feet (107 m)
START/FINISH:	Turn off the A6 at Beetham and park on a short section the old road adjacent to Bela Bridge
GRID REFERENCE:	497797
TERRAIN:	Well defined paths through limestone woodlands and open parkland
NEAREST SHOPS:	Beetham Store
USEFUL MAP:	OS Explorer OL7 English Lakes south east

Prelude

On a fine summer's afternoon, there can be few walks more satisfying than this scintillating venture. A stroll amidst the surging tiers of lime-stone scarring that personify the landscape of North Lancashire is difficult to surpass, and Beetham is the perfect village from which to start.

At one end of the old corpse road from Arnside, coffins were regularly packed over Whin Scar down to the graveyard at Beetham. And no doubt the carriers were more than happy to prop up the bar of the Wheatsheaf Hotel to satisfy a raging thirst. Perhaps we should join their ancestors – but at the end of the walk naturally.

The Walk

To begin, stroll up the back lane towards Dallam Tower passing through a gap-stile after the last house on the left. A short pull up the field with a hedge on your left will bring you to the edge of the woods which are entered by means of another stile.

Then swing immediately right along the wall before slanting up through the trees to a wall-stile abutting an abandoned cottage. What an idyllic retreat this would make for a hermit. However, don't be tempted to enter the precincts which are in danger of imminent collapse.

Bear right to follow a wall around the back garden and on through the trees until a T-junction is reached. Bear right along this major trail soon passing through a wide gap in the crosswall and ignoring all red herrings to right or left. On arriving at a direction cairn keep ahead towards Hazelslack through another wall-gap. The path climbs steadily above a line of moss-clad crags to surmount the domed heights of Whin Scar Woods.

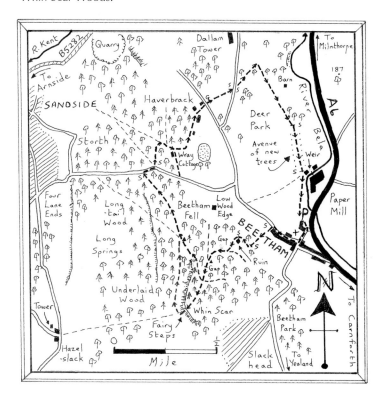

Our route cuts a straight line through the tree cover to emerge into the open at the upper lip of the scar itself. The distant prospect is dominated by Arnside Knott but it is the limestone trench immediately in front that will inevitably draw your attention.

This leads into the constricted rift known as the Fairy Steps and no self-respecting walker can avoid the challenge thrown down by these impish creatures. Descend the narrow stairway to the base of the cliff. Legend says that any wish will be granted, provided of course that you can hop down through the gap without touching the sides. No

Skip carefully down the narrow gap of the Fairy Steps

problem for stick insects, yet even they will have to remove a bulky rucksack. But what about the rest of us? At the bottom, follow the trail down towards Hazelslack for 50 yards (46 m) to descend the second lot of steps. This is much easier and wider. At the bottom of this is a signpost. Head right along the base of the crag to arrive at an open glade and a footpath crossroads.

Keep ahead for a gradual descent through the trees to Cockshott Lane. Bear right for 100 yards (91 m) then pass through a wall-stile into the woods on the opposite side of the lane. Maintain a straight course through the undergrowth, leaning right at a minor T-junction. After passing a signpost, enter a walled track that soon merges with a farm track adjoining Wray Cottage.

Forge onward along this rough lane, which brings you to the hamlet of Haverbrack where the track becomes metalled. On reaching a narrow back lane, cross straight over through a small gate and over the open

The Wheatsheaf Hotel has a superb Tudor-style frontage

field down to the Dallam Tower road. Enter the deer park, stiled at either side, which presents an open prospect with an intermittent scattering of trees.

Aim half left for 200 yards (183 m) passing through a line of beeches. Then swing hard right across a shallow depression between a pair of

The Bela salmon ladder beside Heron corn mill

low knolls, then passing a large barn which should be no more than a 100 yards on the left. You are quite likely to spot the herd of deer for which Dallam is renowned. Be aware that these shy retiring creatures will scoot off if approached.

Mounting the grass banking ahead, keep left of the crest to reach a wall-stile. Then it's downhill all the way to Heron Corn Mill and the Paper Museum between an avenue of trees.

Open between April and September inclusive, both of these interesting places are administered by the large paper mill which is impossible to ignore on the far side of the River Bela.

Built in 1740, the old corn mill was erected on a site of another dating back to 1096. In 1220 the monks of St Marie's Priory of York granted the right to grind corn here. And it is still in operation to this day utilising the power generated by a fourteen foot water wheel.

Close by is a natural ladder for trout and salmon to ascend. A brief walk down the access road will return you to Beetham, and that promised beverage at the pub.

A Walk Worth many Words
Poetry in motion around Rydal Water

DISTANCE:	3.5 miles (5.6 km)
HEIGHT:	300 feet (91 m)
START/FINISH:	If driving from Ambleside, turn left off the A591. After crossing Pelter Bridge, take an immediate right to make use of the free car park 100 yards (91 m) along this road
GRID REFERENCE:	365060
TERRAIN:	Clear paths criss-cross the bracken clad rocky lower slopes that rise up on all sides
NEAREST SHOPS:	Ambleside
USEFUL MAP:	OS Explorer OL7 English Lakes south east

Prelude

Any walk that encircles Rydal Water has to be something of a pilgrimage to the memory of William Wordsworth. One of England's most revered poets, he spent the latter part of his life at Rydal Mount overlooking the lake. All around Rydal, as well as nearby Grasmere, the influence of the great man is difficult to escape. No other person had such a dramatic effect on how the Lake District was perceived in the early nineteenth century.

The poet's cogent observations were eloquently set down in verse which is internationally renowned. Visitors from all corners of the globe come to pay homage to the great man and his revered works. In consequence this is a popular area and not for those who seek to escape from the throngs. But that in no way detracts from its inherent beauty and should not deter you.

And what a superb location it is in the heartland of the National Park, surrounded by craggy heights and rolling foothills. This walk is a circuit of one of the smaller lakes of which Wordsworth was so fond. He spent many idyllic hours on Loughrigg Terrace allowing his imagination to roam free across this delectable landscape. Hemmed by steeply rising fells, the lower though no less exhilarating foothills are suitable for those unable to reach the dizzy heights above.

The Walk

To begin our pilgrimage, make your way up the road beyond the car-park past a couple of houses on your left. Soon afterwards you go through a gate, after which the panorama opens out across Rydal and the wooded foothills beyond towards Grasmere. On the far side, Nab Scar soars aloft, appearing far more grandiose from this angle than is actually the case. Much loftier peaks are concealed from view above and behind. Take the upper track that soon funnels into a walled corridor.

When this opens out, continue ahead past the lower of two major quarries hacked out of Loughrigg Fell's northern flank. Slant left up a winding path to the upper quarry which is infinitely more impressive. A yawning orifice big enough to accommodate the entire population of Ambleside, it is jaw-droppingly spectacular. Much of the slate hewn from this mighty cave was used in the construction of the town.

From here bear left, forking left up a less used path that contours through the bracken carpet above a wood. Eventually it makes a slight descent to join the celebrated Loughrigg Terrace. This is where Wordsworth would spend many an hour admiring the view north across the Vale of Grasmere towards Dunmail Raise. If you have the time, stroll along to the end before returning and taking the lower path down to the end of Grasmere.

A footbridge should be crossed into the wooded enclave that links the two lakes. Turn right to accompany the River Rothay back towards Rydal. After passing another footbridge, make your way up to the main road just beyond the car park at White Moss Common. Cross straight over the main road to continue our walk up the path on the far side.

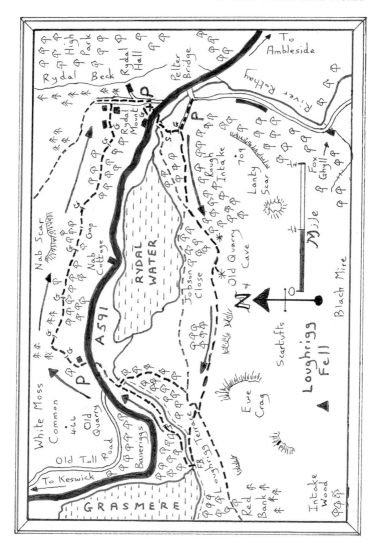

Rydal Mount where William Wordsworth lived

This soon becomes a narrow walled passage which mounts the lower slopes of Nab Scar. The steep cliffs looming ahead form the blunt termination of a ridge spreading south from mighty Fairfield. At the halfway point a gate is passed through. On reaching a walkers' T-junction, bear right along another terraced route. It pursues a delightfully undulating course through a series of gates all the way to Rydal village. The lake appears at intervals through the open woodland cloaking the fellside.

Rydal village, a cluster of farms and cottages, is rather unusual in that it follows a linear pattern at right angles to the main valley. On the right is the magnificent Rydal Mount. Spare some time to investigate this truly enchanting residence that admirably captures the life and times of Lakeland's greatest poet.

Along with the descriptive talent of his sister Dorothy, the Wordsworth legacy is irreplaceable. Much of what has been learned about the great man and his life is down to the dedicated journalistic talents of this unique lady. In addition to poetry, William was a keen explorer. As a physical assessment of the landscape, his Guide to the Lakes *remains a work of deep emotional commitment still considered to be a classic.*

Stroll down the access lane turning right into the church grounds behind which you can access Dora's Field by a stile.

It is a small piece of land purchased by Wordsworth in 1826 when he feared eviction from Rydal Mount, which was only rented at the time. His intention was to build a new house on the land, but when the landlords relented he gave the plot to his daughter. This later passed to his grandson who signed it over to the National Trust in 1935. In spring, the field is a delectable spot carpeted in daffodils and narcissi.

Leave Dora's Field by a gate opening onto the main road and cross over to fork down a narrow passage to reach the banks of the Rothay. Over the footbridge, strike uphill aiming for a wall-stile ahead. Enter some woods mounting a short stairway to gain the old quarry road. Bear left down the lane retracing your steps back to the car park.

Rydal Water with Nab Scar behind

Dora's Field lies behind Rydal church

A Tasty Sandwich Filler
Share a macabre curse with a celebrated walker

DISTANCE:	4 miles (6.4 km)
HEIGHT:	300 feet (91 m)
START/FINISH:	At weekends, make use of the pull-in by the school. Otherwise the main road is wide enough to park on
GRID REFERENCE:	578972
TERRAIN:	Rolling uplands between Lakes and Dales comprising rich grazing pastures
NEAREST SHOPS:	Kendal
USEFUL MAP:	OS Explorer OL7 English Lakes south east

Prelude

In recent times, the name of Grayrigg has received unfortunate national attention due to a bad train derailment nearby. The village itself lies on what was once the main artery connecting Kendal with the old county of Westmorland. The A685 has now been superseded by the M6, so this once-proud highway now mostly serves the local hamlets that litter the area.

Grayrigg is the only village straggling the road between Kendal and Tebay and provides an important focus for rural life in this largely unknown sector of Cumbria – unknown that is unless, like me, you are an avid follower of the much revered fellwalker, Alfred Wainwright.

Half a mile (800 m) to west of the village is the animal rescue sanctuary, set up from proceeds accrued by his famous hand-written guide books to the Lake District. The great AW always claimed that animals were far more deserving of his attention than human beings, who could take care of themselves if in trouble. The centre boasts a modest sign at the entrance and can easily go unnoticed behind a sylvan screen.

The Walk

Our walk begins down a narrow lane at the eastern end of Grayrigg. Take a left fork after 100 yards (91 m) through a gate, ambling down a paved road that drops down to the old farming settlement of Blackett Bottom. Opposite the first house, lean right over a grassy sward to gain a track cutting back alongside a wooded beck.

Immediately after passing the first open gate, slant left down to cross the beck via a solid newly erected footbridge. Mount the facing grass bank to reach a hedge gate, then stride over the next field to another. Thereafter make a sharp left following the hedge on your left over to Green Head. Go through a fenced gap to join the celebrated Dales Way.

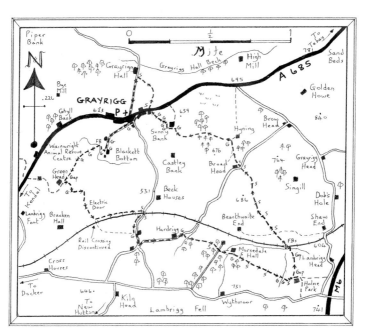

This long-distance footpath stretches 84 miles (135 km) all the way from Bingley in West Yorkshire to Bowness on the shores of Lake Windermere. Keeping to unpaved rights-of-way as much as possible, it normally takes around six days to complete. Next week maybe!

Bear left along a hedged corridor up to a gate, after which a left will carry you down towards another gate. Do not go through this! Instead, lean right across uneven ground aiming for an unusual means of clearing an electric fence stretched across the valley bottom. Wander through what looks like a door frame over which the wire passes. Then stroll up a gentle gradient to reach the main west coast railway line.

Grayrigg Hall conceals a macabre past

The original crossing of the line is now blocked off for safety reasons so head left to reach the first road bridge. On the far side, mount a stile into the field stroll up to a gate to rejoin the road. Take the first left at an offset crossroads and walk down the lane.

Just beyond Hardrigg on the right, go through a gate, followed soon after by another to accompany a fence along to a stile giving access to the wooded grounds of Morsedale Hall. Cross a paved access road, then descend a short but steep banking to cross a bridge, passing right of the second house through a gate.

Beyond a small wood and stile, the path crosses open fields and two more stiles before approaching a double gate. After this watch for a hidden stile in the wall on your left. Walk along the hedge taking the first major gap immediately before Holme Park Farm where we leave the *Dales Way*. Make your way down a pathless slope aiming for the green footbridge that crosses the railway. Just this side of it is a foot-bridge over a stream.

Head for a fence-stile in the top left corner of the field, continuing in a north westerly direction over four more stiles to reach a back lane at Broad Head. Cross straight over, joining a grooved rise after 200 yards (183 m). On reaching a gate near Hyning, aim left along the edge of a large field, then saunter down a passage between two small woods.

This major track leads into the farmyard of Sunny Bank. Bear left around the buildings then right to locate a narrow corridor gated at either end. Still in a constricted flue, wander down a hill through another small gate, passing a garden to gain the main road at the eastern limits of Grayrigg. Slant left for 50 yards (46 m) to locate a stile on the opposite side of the road. Head north making a wide left swing to reach a lane adjacent to Grayrigg Hall.

Before wandering back up the lane to the village, think well on the 'Quaker's Curse' thrown out by Francis Howgill in the year 1660. He claimed to have been unjustly committed to Appleby Jail by Judge Duckett who lived at the Hall. Upon his release, made possible by a bond from fellow Quakers, Howgill went to Grayrigg Hall where he uttered this grim prophecy:

'I am come with a message from the Lord. Thou hast persecuted God's people – but God's hand is now against thee! Thy name shall rot out of the earth, and this house shall become desolate, a habitation for owls and jackdaws!'

Wainwright's shelter for distressed animals

He eventually paid the ultimate price for his faith, dying in prison in 1669. Judge Duckett's family also suffered. By the end of the eighteenth century Grayrigg Hall had become a derelict shell. Thankfully today it has been restored to its former glory.

Ghostly Encounters On The Fell

A dastardly deed &
an aura of mystery

DISTANCE:	4.5 miles (7.2 km)
HEIGHT:	350 feet (107 m)
SUMMIT VISITED:	Cunswick Fell 679 feet (207 m)
START/FINISH:	Just beyond the north Kendal roundabout, turn down the first lane to Burneside. An immediate right on a minor lane offers roadside parking
GRID REFERENCE:	497951
TERRAIN:	Rolling foothills on the edge of the Lake District blend into an eye-catching surge of limestone crags
NEAREST SHOPS:	Burneside
USEFUL MAP:	OS Explorer OL7 English Lakes south east

Prelude

The limestone ridge to the west of Kendal is a favourite spot for locals, and rightly so. It offers an exhilarating wander in open terrain that gives the illusion of being in a far more remote location than is actually the case. The gently shelving approach from the east gives no indication of the dramatic limestone scarring above the Lythe Valley.

This abrupt downfall into the tree-clad fringe is both unexpected and dangerous to the unwary traveller. When viewed at close quarters, or from Whitbarrow across the valley, the rugged grandeur of the escarpment presents a thrilling tableau to the eye. An unusual approach to the ridge is from the north, a circuit that encompasses the true majesty of the fell and its mysterious allure.

The Walk

Set off by crossing the main road where extreme caution is recommended. Go through the stile on the far side. Once you have traversed the field, make a crossing of the access road serving Bannel Head which is stiled at each side. Maintain a parallel course with the hedge some 50 yards (46 m) to your left, heading for a hedge corner ahead.

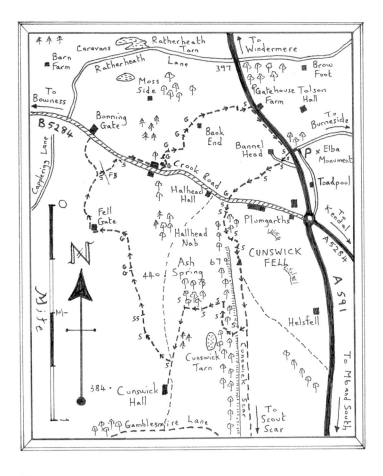

Accompany this to a stile keeping onward but now with the hedge on your right. Go through a gate at the end to cross Crook Road, passing through a gap-stile on the far side.

Cross a small field to enter the lower woods at the northern extremity of Cunswick Fell via a fence-stile. A clear path climbs steadily through the tree cover emerging close to a wall-stile. Beyond this, you come into an upper field so follow the wall around to another stile giving access to the open fell. A short stroll will bring you onto the summit of Cunswick Fell with barely the hint of a sweat raised. The views are stunning.

> But should a grey mantle of cloud descend to cast a gloomy shadow across the open grassy terrain, do not be surprised to witness the fleeting passage of a spectre from the past. This is the ghost of Roger de Leyburne, who stabbed his father in the back to gain the Cunswick estate.
>
> An act of such craven infamy was always bound to be the subject of retribution, and sure enough this happened soon after. One night a hooded figure was seen to enter Roger's chamber without emerging. Next day, Roger was discovered with a knife sticking out of his side. The local priest refused to allow the wicked man to be buried in Kendal churchyard, and so the body was transported back to Cunswick Hall.
>
> As the bearers were carrying the coffin back over the fell, a ferocious storm blew up. The poor fellows were scared stiff that it was a sign from above condemning them for associating with such an evil person. Dropping everything, they fled the macabre scene leaving the coffin on the hillside. What happened thereafter is shrouded in mystery, and has never been fully explained.

From the cairn, head south down a gentle slope towards the distant radio mast. In the depression, watch for a thin path forking right to a stile in the fence that runs along the edge of the steep crag. Go through this into the trees, carefully descending a stony path to the bottom. Two stiles will bring you into an open field.

Aim for a gap in the wall opposite, entering a small wood. Accompany the wall on your left to exit at the far side. Then bear left alongside a wall which should be followed down to Cunswick Hall, the infamous site of Roger de Leyburne's death.

> *On a lighter note, it was also the place where Henry VIII courted his last wife, Catherine Parr. It was in the Corridor of Yews that the King is reputed to have asked for her hand in marriage. This event took place before the original dwelling was pulled down in 1582. The Cunswick Hall that is in evidence today was erected on the site of the hall's old pele tower.*

> *It is around this period that we turn our attention to the fate of another one of the family. James de Leyburne was accused of recusancy for failure to pay allegiance to Queen Elizabeth I by refusing to attend Protestant church services. Such a crime was punishable by a £100 fine, a substantial figure in those days, which he also refused to pay.*

> *Far worse, however, was his public denouncement of the Queen by calling her a usurper of the true faith of Catholicism. For this he was first imprisoned before being despatched to the assizes at Lancaster. Inevitably found guilty, James suffered the brutal method of execution that involves being hung, drawn and quartered.*

> *Unlike others of the de Leyburne family, James might well be considered a brave if stubborn man. It is also worth noting that some months before these tragic events took place, he presented a splendid grandfather clock to the town of Kendal. Could it have been one made by Jonas Barber (see Walk 17)?*

Before reaching the hall, cross over the metalled access road. When I last came this way there was an electric fence-stile to be mounted. Make a half right pathless crossing of this irregular field to reach the wall on the far side where a clear track emerges. Beyond a lonely stile watch for a gated specimen giving access to the adjoining field. Accompany the hedge now on your right, making a diagonal crossing of this field to a gate at the end.

Beware the ghost rider of Cunswick Fell

Another gate immediately in front will find you traversing a wide field, dropping down to a gate at the end where a clear field track is picked up. This will bring you to Fell Gate Farm. Stick with the track through the yard and out the far side. At a gate and cattle grid, mount a wall-stile on the right followed soon after by a slabbed footbridge.

Head north east up a grass slope to reach a wall on Crook Road Head and keep going until you reach a gate hidden from view until the last minute. From here bear right along the road for a quarter mile (402 m), entering the yard of the last building, called High Brundrigg, on the left. Go through the gate to the right of a large stable, circling round behind to the left to reach another gate. Lean right through open trees to a third gate.

Thereafter, swing right across an open stretch, aiming for a small wood in front. Follow this round to the left where a track emerges. Go through a gate and follow the track round with a hedge on your right until you reach another gate at the end. Through this aim half left, mounting a slope past a tree, keeping Bank End on your left to reach a wall-corner.

Fell Gate is a traditional Cumbrian homestead

Henry VIII courted his sixth wife at Cunswick Hall

Now take a due east course across a large open stretch, homing in to the wall at the far corner. Drop down right to another gate where you join a track that leads to the main road by a stile directly opposite Gatehouse Farm. Head right along the grass verge for a quarter mile (402 m) for the return to the start.

A Piece of Heaven on Earth

Tragedy haunts a landscape steeped in charm & serenity

DISTANCE:	3.5 miles (8.6 km)
HEIGHT:	450 feet (137 m)
START/FINISH:	Ample parking available on the access road to St Anthony's Church at Cartmel Fell. Also, just beyond the turn-off for the church is a wide grass verge
GRID REFERENCE:	417879
TERRAIN:	A subdued rolling landscape of Silurian slate cloaked in mixed woodland plantations
NEAREST SHOPS:	High Newton
USEFUL MAP:	OS Explorer OL7 Lake District south east

Prelude

Hidden from view, the gently rolling terrain comprising the Winster Valley is known only to the discerning few. Here you are presented with the opportunity to explore a special corner of Lakeland that can truly be described as a little piece of 'Heaven on Earth'. Even at busy bank holidays, it is unlikely that other walkers will be encountered in this remote spot.

Lying between Lake Windermere and the Lyth Valley, the land settles itself into a series of middle-height moorlands. Neither craggy nor savage with numerous dips and indentations, you can sit for hours alone amidst a surge of scattered woodland glades without encountering another human soul. With only the sheep and birds for company, who could ask for more? Tracks wind through this utopia, affording walks of the highest quality for those seeking an easy afternoon's jaunt away from the high fells.

The finest views, gleaned through intermittent breaks in the sylvan cloak, are to the east where the bold upthrust of Whitbarrow Scar dominates the scene. Take care, for it is easy to become disorientated amidst the undulating charm of Cartmel Fell. Narrow lanes meander through extensive plantations swinging between low craggy knolls where progress is kept to a sedate pace. The brash world of quick-fix immediacy has no place here.

Not to be confused with Cartmel itself, Cartmel Fell lies some miles to the north and has become well known in some circles on account of differing religious associations. Easily passed unnoticed, St Anthony's Church, built in 1504, lies below the fell road and is secreted in a tree-ringed hollow. Inside the small church a powerful sense of history permeates the air.

St Anthony is the patron saint of herdsmen, basketmakers and charcoal burners, occupations that were at one time well represented in this area. Tyson from the old French 'Tisan' meaning 'firebrand', it will come as no surprise to learn that this family surname is the commonest in these dales.

Old carved pews at the front were originally used by the church's benefactor who resided nearby at Swallowmire. Back in the sixteenth century, the Briggs family became wealthy from the sale of wool to Kendal merchants. The first chapel was built for locals who would otherwise have been forced to undertake the exacting journey to Cartmel Priory. Hodge Hill Farm, just below the church with its round chimneys, is a fine example of a farm that spun its own wool yarn on the open galleries that adjoin the house.

The Walk

From the church grounds, stroll back up the paved access road taking a path on the right that will bring you to another lane after 100 yards (91 m). Head right up to the main fell road. Mount the ladder-stile on the opposite side, leaning half left up a shallow bank to reach a wall. On the far side of the stepped wall, a clear path forks right up a steep bank leading to a prominent monument above. Our way lies straight

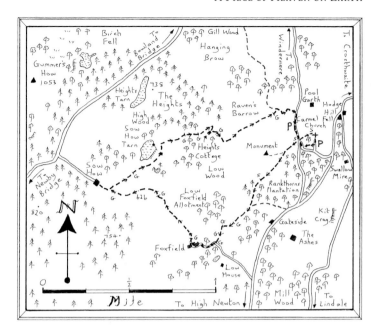

ahead through bracken, entering Rankthorns Plantation by means of a ladder-stile.

Leave the woods at the far side by another stile and soon you will merge with a more prominent track rising from the fell road. Bear right, crossing Spannel Beck and passing through a gate soon after. All around, clumps of trees impede the view, making route direction uncertain. Swing right up a walled passage and through a gate at the top. Slant left, passing through another gate after 100 yards (91 m) before reaching a paved road.

Head right along this road which serves the isolated hamlet of Foxfield. An unusual farming settlement, it is far removed from the general passage of traffic. Beyond the cluster of buildings, the paved road terminates. After passing through a gate, the rough track forges ahead over the open grassy fell.

Whilst wandering across Cartmel Fell you might well hear the haunting lament of a young girl who died hereabouts. Mourning the sad death of her lover, a charcoal burner, from a bolt of lightning whilst sitting outside his hut, the girl refused to leave the spot. Friends brought food but she remained there, constantly calling out his name. Eventually the poor girl succumbed to the cold blast of winter.

A sad reflection as you continue onward through the next gate after which you will find yourself approaching Sow How. Just before the farm, swing right along a track. Go through a fence gate, passing close to the tranquil waters of Sow How Tarn. The path swings left then right through a wall-gap entering Low Wood by a gate. Leave by another at the far side, strolling alongside a wall on your right.

A sharp hairpin to the right will find you nearing Heights Cottage. Once a three-storey residence of some eminence, it is now only used for storage purposes. Accompany a wall to the edge of a small copse, striking through a gate and bearing right onto the open moor of Raven's Barrow. After 100 yards (91 m), make a sharp left to follow a

St Anthony's at Cartmel Fell has an ancient pedigree

Foxfield is an isolated farming hamlet

Pass by the placid reach of Sow How Tarn

grooved track dropping steadily to a wall. Note the monument over to your right with its striking viewpoint.

Through the gate head right down a steepening zigzag to reach the fell road. Head south to a junction, taking the path from here down through the tree cover to the churchyard which lies hidden from view below.

Rather More on the Heath
Papering over the cracks of a still-vibrant industry

DISTANCE:	5 miles (8 km)
HEIGHT:	300 feet (91 m)
START/FINISH:	On the long descent to Staveley, fork left along the old section of road that now offers a good place to park
GRID REFERENCE:	486963
TERRAIN:	Broken heathland that ambles down to the broad sweep of the mid-Kent Valley
NEAREST SHOPS:	Staveley
USEFUL MAP:	OS Explorer OL7 English Lakes south east

Prelude

As they hammer down the long straight beyond the Kendal bypass roundabout, Lakeland visitors are more than likely to miss the old section of road that now acts as a lunch break for local delivery drivers, and likewise the broad expanse of heathland that straddles this south-east boundary of the National Park.

Not the most exciting terrain, boasting little that is Lakeland in character, it is nonetheless a joy to explore. Natural woodland, a hidden gem of a tarn, rough open heath and a river valley second to none; this is the parish known as Strickland Ketel. The nearest settlement of any note is the village of Staveley, itself now bypassed.

Rather Heath is one of those ill-defined parts of Lakeland of which few people are aware. Although the main artery serving Windermere carries vast amounts of traffic, none is ever likely to deviate from this narrow strip of tarmac. Exploration of this little-known terrain is reserved for those discerning walkers who have the good sense and sound judgement to purchase this guide book. In so doing you are unlikely to be disturbed.

The Walk

The section of old road where we are parked adjoining the fringe of Rather Heath Plantation also marks the eastern edge of the Lake District. Take the path on the left, cutting a clear passage through the trees. Beyond a footbridge, cross straight over the tarmac ribbon of Ashes Lane, passing through a stile. Soon after, we arrive at a gate at the edge of the trees and Rather Heath Tarn.

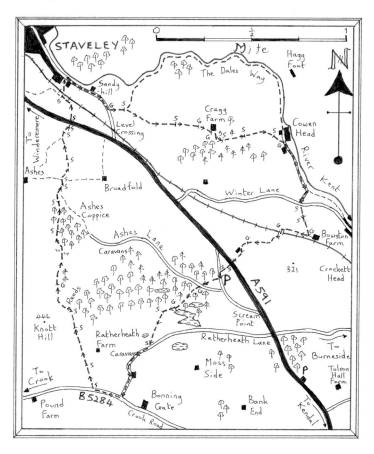

Originally a tiny piece of water, it was extended to its present dimensions by the Cropper Family who still produce paper in the Kent Valley. They wanted a decent stretch to fish at their leisure and filled it with trout. Located in an idyllic setting, it is still a major angling patch today. One gathering of note took place in the early seventeenth century, when James I tried to claim the surrounding farmland for the crown.

Local statesmen farmers considered it their own through right of possession and proceeded to amass a sizeable force to defend this prerogative, by violent means if necessary. Such was their determination that James deemed it wise to accede to their demands and duly backed down.

Veer away from this small stretch, keeping right to locate a step stile in a wall. Then make a half-left traverse of the open grass patch to reach Rather Heath Lane. Bear right along here up to the Crook Road. Another right for a quarter mile will bring you to a footpath signpost pointing the way due north to Staveley.

Mount a stile to accompany the wall on your right as the path makes a slight rise over heathland composed of odd trees and interspersed with gorse and rocky outcrops. After the fourth stile, slant left along a wall to circumvent a marshy tract of reeds. After passing through a wall-gate, the path slants right over to a wall.

Forging onward, keep left of Ashes Coppice to locate a ladder-stile that allows passage through the woods. This area has in the past been utilised for coppicing where the ground shoots of trees are encouraged to promote quick growth. This was to produce charcoal used locally for the smelting of iron.

Coppice woodland on Ratherheath

Leave the wood by a wall-stile, thereafter keeping to the wall on your left for 100 yards (91 m). Then fork away right to the opposite wall-corner which is a right-of-way crossroads. Step over a stile into the field on the right, soon mounting another stile before continuing in a northerly direction down the gently shelving terrain.

Cragg Farm overlooks the Kent Valley

Staveley village is clearly in view ahead in the wide valley bottom. After straddling yet another wall-stile, the path funnels into a narrow walled passage where two stiles bring us out onto the Staveley bypass. Take care when crossing as vehicles are travelling fast along this busy highway.

On the far side, keep to the wall on your left to reach the railway. A walled corridor leads down to a bridge allowing passage beneath. Bear left through a farm yard to gain the old road into Staveley.

Now a sleepy village housing commuters, it was once a major source of bobbins for the textile industry, with five water-powered mills employing many people.

Close by is a pub called the Eagle and Child. The legend concerning the origin of its name stems from the reign of Edward III. Sir Thomas Lathom's wife had failed to produce a son, which drove the frustrated noble into the arms of a local farmer's daughter, who inevitably found herself with child.

The girl gave birth to a boy which prompted Thomas to leave the child in a basket close by a path where his wife took her daily constitutional. This lady believed her husband's cunning assertion that the boy had been stolen by an eagle which had dropped its prey after being disturbed. Adopting the child as their own, the family brought him up as a worthy heir.

Head right away from the village for a quarter mile (402 m) before slanting left through a gate down a narrow corridor. At the end it is decision time. If you enjoy riverside walks then mount the stile and follow the course of the celebrated Dales Way down to the banks of the Kent.

Otherwise, keep right along a passage hemmed in by an interesting archway of trees. At its end, mount a wall-stile and aim diagonally on a due-east bearing over a smooth grass field. Lean in to the tree cover to pass through a gate and along a field track to reach Cragg Farm. Go through the upper gate to join the farm access road.

On the far side is a stile allowing passage over the garden to another that deposits you in a rough tract comprising a loose cloak of trees. Keep heading east down a steepening slope to the edge of the open woodland where a stile is crossed. You are now leaving the Lake District to descend a field towards the old paper mill at Cowan Head.

The enclosed nature of the Kent Valley makes this river a powerful force that was ideal for water power. This potent vigour unfortunately caused severe flooding in 2009.

Where population ratios are considered, there were four times the number of mills in this remote northern enclave during the

Industrial Revolution than in Birmingham. This situation did, however, change radically with the advent of steam power.

Mills sited along the Kent at Bowston and Burneside specialised in paper manufacture. The first mill was built at Cowan Head by Thomas Ashburner in 1760 and made lower quality general paper, the high quality product still being concentrated in Burneside in a large modern factory.

Go through a stile taking note of the original cottages of this industrial hamlet to your left. Pass through a gate further down to gain the road, passing this renovated complex of modern apartments. At the head of the access road bear left to cross Winter Lane, where a stile allows continuation over the next field half left to a stile and thence to Bowston Hall.

Pass through a gate to the right of the farm, heading right up a walled track to cross the railway and so up to the main road. Cross straight over for a short walk on the right of a wall back to the old road stiled at either end of the path.

Cowan Head was once a thriving paper mill

Tickling the Trout

Explore the parish of the crafty shepherding cleric

DISTANCE:	4 miles (6.4 km)
HEIGHT CLIMBED:	400 feet (122 m)
START/FINISH:	Turn off the A592 just before Troutbeck Church along a side lane and park on the left beside the beck
GRID REFERENCE:	412028
TERRAIN:	The lower reaches of the Troutbeck Valley display the classic glaciated form of steep sides and a flat floor
NEAREST SHOPS:	Troutbeck Post Office
USEFUL MAP:	OS Explorer OL7 English Lakes south east

Prelude

Avoided by the main road from Windermere over Kirkstone Pass, the village of Troutbeck became a prosperous community under the patronage of yeoman farmers during the seventeenth century. Our walk does not take in the main village street that follows a spring line, although it is well worth a visit at some other time after you have completed Walk 35.

On the main road to our left is the slate-built Jesus Church. Dating from the 16th century, it was replaced in 1736 and renovated in 1828. A consecrated church was deemed necessary by the Bishop of Chester to avoid the hazardous coffin journey down to St Martins in Windermere. In spring, serenity and peace of mind within the church-yard are complemented by an extensive display of daffodils. There is also a war memorial to be admired which is hewn from a single block of stone.

Troutbeck clerics from a past generation were known to subsidise their meagre retainers by working as shepherds. This brings to mind the story of a certain vicar of Troutbeck who met the Bishop of Carlisle whilst moving his sheep along the main street. When asked directions to the Parsonage, our worthy described the longer route to the bishop who then proceeded on his way.

Meanwhile, the vicar was able to get back to his abode and regale himself in the appropriate vestments to receive his guest. One can but surmise as to what the bishop's reaction would have been had he recognised the parson.

The Walk

At the junction of the main road head right in the direction of Windermere. Cross over to enter a constricted passage that climbs steeply out of the valley. This is stony underfoot and overhung by trees in its lower extremity. Pass through a gate close to The Howe, after which the track continues ahead for 100 yards (91 m) then veers sharply to the left. After this, the gradient eases.

At an offset walkers' crossroads abutting a small cluster of trees, fork left through a gate to take the lower path. The main track continues ahead on its upward perambulation towards Garburn Pass. This route is the main link with Kentmere. Our path makes a gradual descent into the lower reaches of the Troubeck Valley.

Pursuing a direct course slightly east of north the route virtually arrow straight, just like the valley. A straggly line of hawthorn trees provides a guard of honour on the left as we pass the extensive outdoor leisure facilities of Limefitt Park. At the northern end of the park is a slope where grass skiing takes place, and a chair lift has been provided for skiers.

Immediately beyond pass through a gate, continuing onward towards the white farmstead of Long Green Head. Ahead can be seen a rising wedge of rock occupying the centre of the valley known as Troutbeck Tongue. Soon after passing the farm, watch for a gate on the left which is the access track linking up to the valley road.

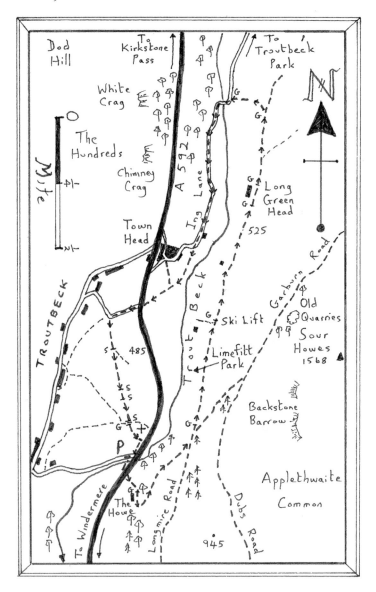

Bear left along the road, soon crossing Trout Beck via Ing Bridge for the return walk down valley. The high fells at the head of the valley afford an exhilarating trek for another day. But from Troutbeck, the way is long and encompasses the unfrequented upper reaches of the valley.

For an easy-going stroll on a fine spring day, this short ramble makes for an ideal introduction to this delectable locale. Indeed, when the sun shines and the birds are in full song, there can be no better means of spending a fruitful day. Choose a midweek visit as Troutbeck is a deservedly popular tourist attraction in summer.

Just beyond a stone barn, Ing Lane veers sharp right for the climb up to the hamlet of Town Head. Our way continues straight ahead along a narrow walled passage. It climbs gradually to join the main road which we cross to stroll up a metalled lane. After 200 yards (183 m) this turns to the right at an unusual cross-roads where two of the arms are rough tracks.

Spring daffodils flourish around the Jesus Church

A right here would take you up to the main street at the northern end of Troutbeck village. Here stands the Mortal Man Hotel. Built in 1869 it was originally called the White House Inn. This amusing rhyme makes fun of the poet's over-indulgent companions:

> *Mortal Man, that lives by bread,*
> *What is it makes thy nose so red?*
> *Thou silly fool, that looks 't so pale,*
> *'Tis drinking Sally Birkett's ale.*

Unless you also want to make an acquaintance with the amber nectar, take a left here. Accompany the wall on the right until a hurdle is reached and the track slants away to the left. Look out for a stile hidden from view until the last moment on the right. Amble along the enclosed grass track which soon funnels into a metre-wide fenced corridor. Pass through two stiles near together on a banking above a tributary feeding into Trout Beck.

Continuing the gradual descent, a stile at the bottom deposits us on a major track once used by the villagers for attending the church services. Cross straight over this through a white gate and so into the churchyard. Exit on the far side through a lychgate heading right back to the car park.

Visit the Mortal Man in Troutbeck

In Step with a Moonshiner

Illicit hooch & slate quarrying make for strange bedfellows

DISTANCE:	4 miles (6.4 km)
HEIGHT:	400 feet (122 m)
START/FINISH:	Take the left fork signposted for Wrynose Pass at the head of Little Langdale. Limited parking is available after 100 yards (91 m) on the right
GRID REFERENCE:	301033
TERRAIN:	Constricted at its entrance, Little Langdale opens out to display the classic proportions of a glaciated valley with steep sides and a flat floor
NEAREST SHOPS:	Elterwater
USEFUL MAP:	OS Explorer OL7 English Lakes south east

Prelude

Little Langdale enjoys a certain aloof detachment when compared to its larger cousin to the north on the far side of Lingmoor Fell. The tiny village with its narrow winding road endeavours to dissuade onward progression at every turn. Motorists are, therefore, deterred from lingering, continuing onward over Wrynose Pass or up to Blea Tarn. In consequence, there is a dearth of fellow ramblers with whom to pass the time of day. I for one prefer it that way.

It is the remoteness and inaccessiblity of the valley that encouraged the illicit production of whiskey in the past. What a daunting task it must have been for excisemen in the last century struggling to catch up with will o' the wisp moonshiners who quickly disappeared with their fiery tipple like a breath of wind.

Most colourful and productive of the clandestine distillers was Lancelot Slee. Known as Lanty he began his 'spiritual' career at Low Colwith around the middle of the nineteenth century. The name is derived from Norse meaning cunning, clever and sly, a very apt moniker for the rascally Mr Slee.

Stills producing a continuous output of the potent brew were scattered throughout the district to protect them from the unannounced visits from the revenue men. The illicit brew from locally grown potatoes was much sought after by all sections of the community, including magistrates who were not averse to tipping the wink should a raid be in the offing.

But not all raids proved to be fruitless ventures. One such conviction by the Hawkshead magistrates cost the roguish fellow £150 in 1853, which was the equivalent of three years wages' to the ordinary farm labourer. It shows how much profit there was in this illegal trade. After this, prospective consumers erred on the side of caution by enquiring if Lanty had harvested 'a good crop of taties this year'.

The Walk

From the parking area close to the Blea Tarn fork, continue along the road in the direction of Wrynose Pass. Watch for a stile on the left where we cross to the far side of the valley. First, however, a short detour further along the Wrynose road will bring us to Fell Foot Farm.

Directly above the front door is an overhanging room supported by pillars. This was used by Lanty Slee to store copious gallonage of his potent elixir.

The farmer's wife was once challenged by excisemen whilst carrying the brew in a pig's bladder beneath her capacious skirt. The rest had already been hidden. She managed to browbeat the officers into effecting a less than adequate search and they were forced to leave empty-handed. A near miss that resulted in Lanty and his confederates enjoying a celebratory skinful.

Now return to the stile. At the far side of the valley, cross Geenburn Beck via a sturdy footbridge, passing Bridge End Cottage on the left.

The track bends left climbing gradually to pass through another stile. A major track once used by miners heading up the Greenburn Valley is soon joined.

Keep to an easterly course down valley passing through a gate close to a cottage. The track then veers sharp left downhill passing Low Hall Garth which is owned by the Yorkshire Ramblers. Passing beneath the spoil tips of the old quarries rising up on our right, the finest view is over to the left where Little Langdale Tarn sparkles in the sunlight, if you are lucky.

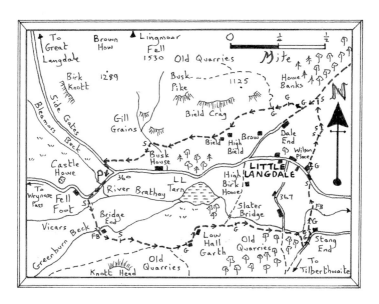

Passage to the opposite side of the valley is by means of the ancient packhorse crossing appropriately named Slater Bridge. There are many such examples of these low yet sturdy structures around Lakeland. Their continued use after many centuries testifies to the skilful construction by our forebears. The short detour to admire this centuries-old feature is highly recommended.

Slaters: a classic example of a packhorse bridge

Then carry on accompanying the River Brathay up to a crossing of tracks by a wooden footbridge. Keep ahead on a narrow path that soon leans right away from the river to join a metalled cross road. Bear left up the hill to reach Stang End.

Go through the gate on the left and make your way down a walled passage, passing through two more gates to cross the river below by a footbridge. The path on the far side points the way to the main valley road. Head left towards Little Langdale village slanting right after 100 yards (91 m) by a white cottage. Go past Wilson Place through a gate at the rear.

A clear path accompanies a new fence on your left. Leading into a narrow corridor stiled at each end, the path then makes a sharp dogleg crossing open ground to join the main track linking this valley with Elterwater. Head left but watch for a gate on the right after 100 yards (91 m). This path mounts the valley side on a well-graded course passing through two more gates.

After this we begin the descent on a splendid high-level route that follows the steep southern face of Lingmor Fell, keeping the intake wall on your left until a deep gorge is crossed lower down. Here the path swings to the left over a stile. With the wall now on your right, the path proceeds across a level shelf of rock back to the Blea Tarn road. A left followed by a right down a stony track will return you to the car.

The famous overhang at
Fell Foot Farm

Wetherlam stands guard
over Little Langdale

Bowled Over by a Grandfather

Savour the enthralling appeal of a forgotten landscape

DISTANCE:	5.5 miles (8.6 km)
HEIGHT:	300 feet (91 m)
START/FINISH:	Take the Lythe Valley road from Windermere forking right at Winster. Drive for a mile as far as the rough access track serving Wood Farm then park on the grass verge close to the River Winster
GRID REFERENCE:	413916
TERRAIN:	Low undulating hills cloaked in woodland to the east of Windermere
NEAREST SHOPS:	Bowland Bridge
USEFUL MAP:	OS Explorer OL7 English Lakes south east

Prelude

Tucked away to the east of Windermere, a series of low inter-connecting valleys provide stimulating walks of the highest quality. Dense tree cover abounds which makes their forms rather indistinct. Unlike the more open dales for which Lakeland is famous, the Winster Valley has more in keeping with that of the Duddon.

Narrow lanes swoop and dive amidst the rustic scenery, enclosing the visitor in a fascinating world of timeless appeal. A curious situation is encountered here trying not to get lost amidst the enclosed sylvan world. A map was essential to actually locate where I wanted to park. Barely two miles from the bustling shores of Lake Windermere, yet a million distant in essence and tranquillity, Winster will always remain a firm favourite of mine.

Entering this labyrinth is like stepping back in history, back to an age of gentility when man had time for himself. Just like the river which gently meanders south to join the Kent near to Grange-over-Sands. Spring is the season when Winster and her environs come alive, new life bursting forth with oceans of daffodils and bluebells providing a gloriously colourful carpet.

It is hard to imagine that in the 1960s there was a suggestion made that the Winster Valley would fall prey to the insatiable demand for Lakeland water – a fate that other, less fortunate, valleys were forced to suffer. Thankfully, common sense prevailed and this delectable corner of Heaven on earth can be enjoyed by all who are prepared to venture off the beaten track.

The Walk

We start off by wandering up the narrow lane to the Birks Bridge ford.

Locked within the embrace of dense woodland, consider this story from days of yore. At that time of the Crusades, the woodland carpet extended unbroken all the way to the shores of Lake Windermere to such an extent that squirrels were able to cover the entire span without touching the ground.

Within this densely forested area lived a ferocious wild boar, whose depravations exacted a heavy toll on the local populace. Wanton and capricious, the savage beast had done away with numerous victims before disappearing into the woods back to his secret lair. Nobody dared go out alone for fear of being savaged by the rampant creature.

In the neighbouring valley lived Richard de Gylpin, a Norman knight who had acquitted himself honourably in the Holy War. He was determined to rid the district of this dangerous swine. The thick woodland made it extremely difficult to track his quarry down, but in earnest he persisted. Eventually, his torrid endeavour came to a head in a ferocious battle with the brute.

Back and forth raged the combatants, each seeking to gain the initiative. Much blood was spilled by both as the deadly duel neared its climax. Although severely wounded, our heroic paladin was able to make the fatal thrust that despatched the snarling boar to its happy hunting grounds.

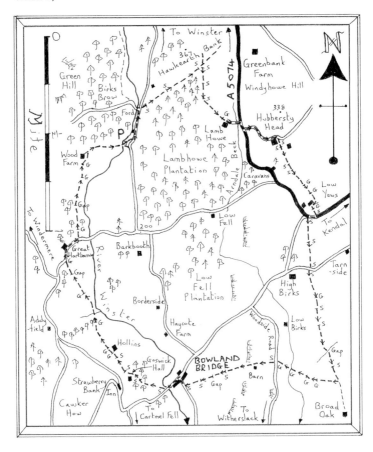

The epic contest was immortalised in the family coat of arms which hung for many years in Scaleby Castle north of Carlisle where the De Gylpins once lived. Clearly the family exerted significant influence over medieval Cumbria, the name cropping up all over the county.

Pause at the road junction. Here the river takes priority, submerging the road for a considerable distance. No problem for pedestrians who are provided with a solid stone fixture. This is clearly a feature dating back to a time when horse-drawn vehicles were the sole means of propulsion. On this walk, we do not use the footbridge.

Instead, bear right to head north east up rising ground on the left side of a wall. Cresting the shallow vale over Hawkearth Bank, we swing sharp right after the third stile to cross another now heading due south along the edge of woodland. Beyond a broken wall, watch for a ladder-stile offering access to a fenced passage in the woods.

Exiting at the far end into a field, stroll down to the farmstead of Lamb Howe. The access road leads down to the main road. This is the valley of Arndale Beck. Bear right then left up a narrow lane to

Birks Bridge allows pedestrians to cross the Winster

Hubbersty Head. Just beyond the house, lean right over a wall-stile. Another soon after brings you out into rolling grassy terrain.

Maintain a south-south-easterly bearing to the field corner and a double stile. The next stile takes you into the adjoining field on the left. Now aim directly for Low Yews. Circle right past the cottages then leave the track to head left through a gate down to reach the main road again. Head right for 100 yards (91 m) before entering the field on the far side.

Still heading south, crest a low knoll to reach the right of two wall-gaps. The step stile is on the left for onward transit down to a back lane. Cross straight over, continuing south through a gate and two more stiles to reach a wide gap in the wall. Step over a stream and aim for the middle of the following wall and another stile.

You can now see a clear track heading west to gain Woodside Road. Westward progression is via a stile offset to the left. Mount a low bank keeping right of a prominent barn to cross the nobbly crest and walk down hill back into the Winster Valley. A direct course along the edges of three walled fields will bring you to a road close to Bowland Bridge.

There is no mistaking the dominance of the hotel, dwarfing as it does this tiny settlement. But the village is more well known in horological circles as the place where Jonas Barber practised the craft of building precision grandfather clocks in the eighteenth century. His son continued the family business following Jonas's death and fine examples of their work are to be found all over the country to this day.

Head right to a junction and the key focus point in the whole area. Bear left here to cross the river bridge, leaning immediately right through a gate stile. Cross open ground to enter rocky woodland through a broken wall-gap. Yellow marks point the way past the lower edge of Goswick Hall.

The old farming community of Hubbersty Head

Jonas Barber made clocks at Bowland Bridge

Above and behind is the Mason's Arms at Strawberry Bank. Celebrated hereabouts and beyond for its array of locally brewed ales, it also produces a distinctive and potent damson gin. We now head north west towards the farmstead of Hollins. Keep left of the buildings along a walled track and you will soon be paralleling the River Winster which joins from the right. Maintain a NNW bearing to reach the back lane at Great Hartbarrow.

Swing right down here for 273 yards (250m), heading left at the next signpost. Go through a gate aiming due north to a gap on the right of some woods. When the wall veers away left, keep ahead over a flat field, passing through two more gates to reach Wood Farm. A short stroll right down the access track will return you to the River Winster and a parked car.

Where We Come In

A tribute to Cumbria's favourite walker

DISTANCE:	6 miles (9.7 km)
HEIGHT:	450 feet (137 m)
SUMMIT VISITED:	Orrest Head 783 feet (239 m)
START/FINISH:	Ample roadside parking available at the junction of Moorhowe and Dubbs Road
GRID REFRENCE:	424006
TERRAIN:	The knobbly eastern flank of the Troutbeck Valley culminates in a perky rise at Orrest Head
NEAREST SHOPS:	Windermere
USEFUL MAP:	OS Explorer OL7 English Lakes south east

Prelude

As the celebrated Lakeland walker Alfred Wainwright said on first ascending Orrest Head in 1930, this is 'where we come in.' And his assertion still applies today. Although rather insignificant in stature, Orrest Head is the first fell encountered by most people who arrive at Windermere. And as was the case with Wainwright, it might well be their first experience of the glorious pastime that is fell wandering.

Overlooking the town from the north, the great man was hooked from the very start. Surrounded by woodland, the final breakthrough above the tree level offers what Wainwright said was his 'first sight of mountains in tumultuous array across glittering waters, our awakening to beauty.' Indeed there can be few other viewpoints that present such a perfect tableau, the meeting of all that is best in utopian harmony.

Wainwright certainly felt the unique aura of the place, and who am I to disagree? Neither will you when surveying the most majestic of panoramas from behind the view indicator. Like thousands before you,

you can stand silently in awe of the sheer enchantment created by mother nature, before reclining on one of the host of seats provided for a well-earned lunch. And all this is afforded by a small oasis that would be swallowed up whole if relocated in the heart of the District.

The Walk

Our walk begins from the fell road linking Troutbeck and Ings – a shortcut avoiding Windermere. Head north along a broad walled track called Dubbs Road. It eventually merges with the Garburn Road, continuing on up to the renowned pass of the same name.

Climbing gradually, we pass the extensive Dubbs reservoir as the track contours around the lower slopes of Applethwaite Common. These rough highways were once important thoroughfares for the transit of goods and people in the district. They offer a good indication of the difficulties encountered by early residents when moving from one area to another in their daily lives.

When the track dips and just before a small copse, watch for a ladder-stile on the left. A grass path drops down to join the walled Garburn Road below. Head left down to a walkers' crossroads, forking left up a slight gradient along Longmire Road. We are now on the ancient Roman road connecting Ambleside with Brougham near Penrith. The

Enjoy the view over Troutbeck from Dubbs Road

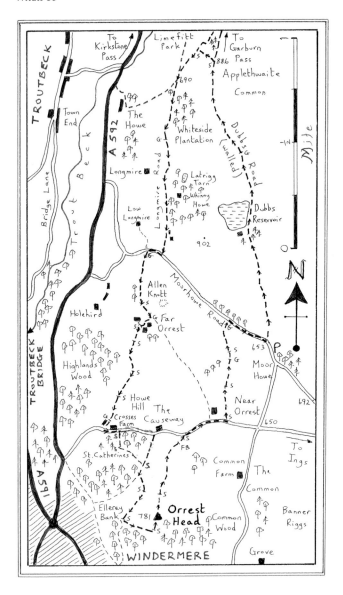

upper section of this is the famed High Street. The final quarter mile (402 m) before rejoining Moorhowe Road is paved.

Bear right downhill for 100 yards (91 m), slanting left through a gate to follow a grooved track around the lower reaches of Allen Knott. Unseen from this situation are the remnants of the old Iron Age hill fort. Home in to pass through a gap, keeping the wall on your right up to a stile.

A walled passage will bring you to a halt just before the farming hamlet of Far Orrest. This cluster of old cottages gives a sound idea of how many Lakeland settlements grew up in times past. Go through the gate on the right and across a small pasture to a stile at the far side. Over the access road is another stile. Then lean to the left, leaving this somewhat confusing amalgam of stone cottages to accompany a clear track south to another gate.

Beyond this follow a wall round to the left. Another two stiles and a gate will find you entering another local hamlet known as Crosses. Comprising a selection of cottages and slate houses, the original was built in 1558. It has been suggested that the name refers to a preaching cross that must have been here at one time. Originally called Crosshouse, it could refer to a medieval chapel nearby that was dedicated to St Catherine, who has also given her name to the woods alongside.

Head left along a back lane for 50 yards (46 m) up to a stile on the right giving access to the Low Hag Wood owned by the National Trust. Follow the path through the woods up to another stile, after which swing left uphill on the edge of the woods accompanying a wall on your left up to a signposted stile. This section is a new path that has replaced that from The Causeway, the white building seen a quarter mile (402 m) down to your left. For some unaccountable reason it was closed in September 2007.

From here head right, forking left up to a stile higher up. From here the path then drops down to enter the woods of Elleray Bank. Make an immediate sharp left up a stepped path and then along a wall/fence

Ann takes up the Wainwright pose on
Orrest Head

Religious connotations have been attached to
Crosses

passage. At the end, swing left pausing to read the carved inscriptions.
There follows a short pull onto the summit of Orrest Head and the
promised view that only a mist-shrouded day can spoil.

> *One of the earliest acquisitions of the National Trust, Orrest
> Head was donated by Arthur Heywood in 1902. The name
> suggests that a major battle was fought here in the dark ages.
> Later it was given over to extensive grain farming prior to the
> Enclosure Act of 1831 that created the network of grazing fields
> now in existence.*

Wordsworth extolled the view in his epic poem *The Prelude*. At some
point you will have to drag yourself away from this small piece of
Heaven, so head north down a slope through heather to cross a wall-
stile below. Stick close to the wall on your left all the way down to a
small clutch of conifers. A slabbed footbridge is soon followed by a
stile giving onto the fell road.

Lean right for a quarter mile (402 m), keeping alert for a wall-stile
located one hundred metres beyond the entrance to Near Orrest.
Here you should traverse a field to mount a ladder-stile. Then keep to
a straight course over a pathless grass pasture, passing through a gate
in the wall.

Still heading due north, cross the next short field to a stile. Accompany
the wall on your left as it swings to the right returning you to Moorhowe
Road. A right will see you back at the parking spot.

Gorging on Iron

Step back into a landscape dominated by relics of its industrial heritage

WALK 19

DISTANCE:	6.5 miles (10.5 km)
HEIGHT:	350 feet (107 m)
START/FINISH:	At the end of the Leven Gorge, fork left off the main road into the village of Haverthwaite. Then left again after half a mile (800 m) along the B5278. Ample parking is available on the right just beyond the entrance to Birk Dault
GRID REFERENCE:	345834
TERRAIN:	The Leven has carved a spectacular exit to the sea through a gap in the undulating slate uplands of South Lakeland
NEAREST SHOPS:	Greenodd
USEFUL MAP:	OS Explorer 0L7 English Lakes south east

Prelude

The subdued fell country around Backbarrow and Haverthwaite comprises Silurian slates that are less resistant to erosion than the harder rocks that typify the core of the Lake District. Low level rolling terrain cloaked in extensive tracts of woodland characterises these fells. At this southern extremity, the heights plunge quite steeply down to meet the coastal plain, distinguished by flat extensively drained mosslands.

The scattered nature of Haverthwaite makes it difficult to pin down as a village. It does, however, have one claim to fame in that the cele-brated children's writer Arthur Ransome lived here. His adventure stories are intertwined with the Lakeland landscape he revered so much. Today it is known mainly for the preserved section of railway along which steam trains operate.

The Walk

Our walk begins at the foot of the abrupt escarpment known as Bigland Heights. Having escaped from the open expanse of Windermere, the River Leven has taken advantage of a weakness in the rock formation to carve out a magnificent gorge. We join the river where it debouches from its constricted passage by walking back up the road to Low Wood Bridge.

Bear left downstream then right after 100 yards (91 m) through a stile to follow the river bank. We pass through another stile beside a clump of trees, continuing straight ahead to cut off a sharp bend. A footbridge and stile will then find us once again accompanying the river up to the farm access road beside Fish House. Head right for a mile (1.6 km) until Roundsea Wood is reached. Watch for a narrow path branching right, which brings us to the point where the old railway crosses the river.

> *This was a branch line from Ulverston to Lakeside for early tourists wishing to join the lake steamer. Opened by the Furness Railway in 1868, only a three-mile section now remains operating from Haverthwaite Station.*

Cross the river and stroll up this abandoned track for 100 yards (91 m) until a stile on the left allows you to continue along the river bank. The path sits atop an embankment that branches right after half a mile (800 m) to accompany the tributary of Rusland Pool. Cross over the main road, continuing on the far side. The path is indistinct but the course obvious. After half a mile (800 m) we arrive at a road known as The Causeway.

Bear right along here for a quarter mile (402 m) until a gate is reached on the right. The right-of-way is pathless but makes a direct beeline for the far corner of the moss after crossing a footbridge. Mount a stile here to enter a narrow passage that climbs up a shale slope to join a back lane. Slant left for 200 yards (183 m) until a lane breaks right up a gentle slope.

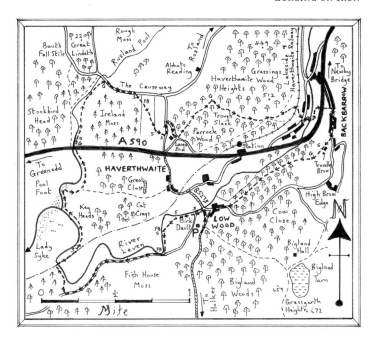

On reaching the buildings at Lane Ends, watch for a path on the left. This enters Parrack Wood, climbing steadily to pass through a high gated fence. Keep onward as the path becomes walled. The amusing story is told of a mysterious little prankster with pointed ears and a long red nose who roams these woods in summer knocking the hats off passers-by. Dressed entirely in green, he then disappears into the leafy foliage. You are advised, therefore, to remove any headgear while passing through these woods!

At its top end, lean right immediately after passing through the exit gate. The path now skirts the upper reaches of Haverthwaite Heights passing two charcoal-burning sites.

Woodland in this area has developed along the lines of 'coppicing', which involves cutting trees down to ground level to

101

produce thin shoots. When cut, these are quickly regrown, unlike fully mature trees which take years. The aim was to preserve tree growth which was fast diminishing in the eighteenth century due to heavy demands made by the burgeoning iron industry. Oak, ash, birch and hazel, which dominate the woodland scene, were ideal for charcoal manufacture, an essential ingredient for the smelting of locally mined iron ore.

Perhaps some knowledgeable reader could enlighten your guide as to why charcoal is still being produced today. Fuel for barbecues is all that springs to mind, unless it is to help preserve the tradition of a past heritage by dedicated enthusiasts.

Soon after the second charcoal burner, the path descends the south-facing slope of the Heights towards Backbarrow. Keep with the main footpath avoiding any permissive extras. This will bring you down to the railway. Cross with care then join the old valley road. Backbarrow was once an important iron-smelting village, founded in 1711. Remains of the iron works can be seen along the river bank if you look closely.

Steam trains operate from Haverthwaite to Lakeside

A sturdy bridge spans Rusland Pool

Gunpowder used to be made at
Low Wood

Bear left then right to cross the Leven via a footbridge. The continuing footpath goes under the new road, climbing up to join the rest of Backbarrow which was sliced in two by the bypass. Bear right up the hill to the higher settlement of Low Brow Edge, forking right down a path sign-posted to Trundle Brow. Join the footpath leading back down to valley level through a gap-stile. The clear path will take you down through the trees to Low Wood.

> *A cluster of slate cottages adjoins a preserved slate works boasting a fine clocktower. Established in 1799, the works made use of local charcoal in the manufacture of gunpowder. It made use of ash charcoal in the process, most of which was used for blasting in the mines around Coniston. New explosives such as dynamite effectively sealed the fate of a local industry based on dwindling supplies of charcoal. The industry finally came to an end shortly after the First World War. By that time, gunpowder production from charcoal had been moved to Scotland by ICI who had taken over most of the sites.*

From Low Wood, take the left fork to rejoin the road for a short stroll back to the start.

A Walk Requiring a Slack Rein

Where the White Lady & a Royalist spy join hands

DISTANCE:	6.5 miles (10.5 km)
HEIGHT:	400 feet (122 m)
START/FINISH:	Pull off the A590 at Witherslack parking anywhere along the old road beyond the Derby Arms
GRID REFERENCE:	441828
TERRAIN:	Heavily wooded limestone uplands with deeply entrenched valleys between
NEAREST SHOPS:	Witherslack otherwise Lindale Village
USEFUL MAP:	OS Explorer OL7 English Lakes south east

Prelude

Witherslack and Winster are two of the most delightful valleys in the Lake District. They are completely at odds with classic expectation, of how such terrain ought to appear. No soaring rugged peaks that hurtle skywards reaching for the clouds. No lakes and wide open views across a mountainous landscape. What the area does have in abundance is solitude and a timeless appeal that is enhanced by its peacefulness.

Extensive woodland contributes markedly to a feeling that progress has passed by unheeded. Around every corner there is something to enrich the soul and stimulate the mind. A slower pace of life pertains here, unfettered by the claims of modern technology. Narrow winding lanes that tortuously meander across a subdued arena slow traffic down to a crawl that is very much in keeping with the character of the place.

Tiny villages go about their business unconcernedly, white-washed and slatey. And as the revered Millom writer Norman Nicholson once astutely observed, 'Here is a sign of what the Lake District might still be if the rest of England had not got to know about it.'

Savour this relatively unknown locale at your leisure. There is no sign here of the hustle and bustle of contemporary life, nor is it welcomed.

The Walk

The old road, now long since abandoned and becoming grassed over in places, offers a poignant start to our walk. Join the new road turning hard right immediately beyond the services to follow a clear track. Beyond the first stile, lean away from the walled woods. The path heads down a slight rise to re-enter heavily coppiced woodland beside a ruin with a stile and wall-gap in close proximity.

Heading in a NNW direction along a narrow footpath, ignore all other paths forging off to right and left. Maintain a direct course passing through various gaps and stiles to reach the first house on the edge of Witherslack village. This scattered settlement is oddly located in the Winster Valley, straggling over a low shoulder into the neighbouring vale.

Cross a road and through a small iron gate, swinging immediately left to follow a fence round to the village's northern limit. Pass between a hotel and the church.

The old schoolhouse was endowed by the Reverend John Barwick in 1664. A staunch royalist at the time of the Civil War, he was removed from office under the orders of Oliver Cromwell and forced into hiding. Refusing to be subdued, Barwick became a spy for King Charles I. Eventually he was caught and imprisoned, his goods impounded by the state. Not until the restoration of the crown by Charles II were the doughty cleric's fortunes restored. Upon his return to Witherslack, Barwick was so distressed by the neglected state of his church and grounds by the Catholic landlords (the Leyburne Family – see Walk 12) that he commissioned a new church to be built.

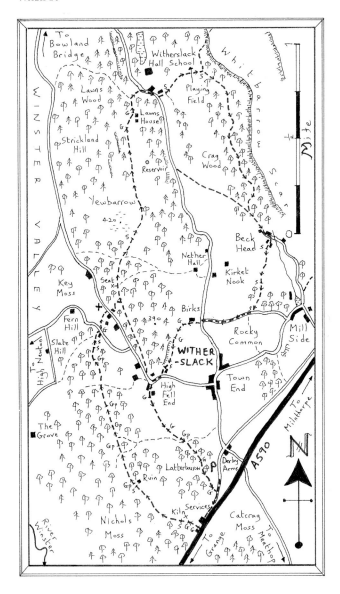

The White Lady walks the corridors of Witherslack Hall

In addition, dowries were left for the poor maids of the parish, the money also being used for a new burial ground to be consecrated. Thus the long and protracted journey of carrying the deceased to the nearest graveyard at Beetham was avoided (see more in Walk 2). John Barwick was a philanthropist who clearly felt it was his bounden duty to improve the lot of his flock. And for that he is to be highly commended.

From the environs of the church, cross straight over the road to mount a steeply canting path. This climbs in a series of zigzags uphill to merge with the main crossfell track. Head left through the tree cover until a fork in the trail after 200 yards (183 m).

At this point, swing away to the left through the tree cover to emerge onto the abrupt limestone edge. Here a magnificent open prospect stretches across the lower Winster to the slate ridge of Newton Fell on the far side. A stone seat laid in AD 2000 has been provided to enjoy the view at your leisure.

Returning to the main path continue onward, emerging into an open common through a gate stile. We are now crossing Yewbarrow, which is the highest point on this side of the Witherslack Valley. Aim half right down a gentle gradient to a wall where the clear trail heads due north, crossing a grassy pasture gated at each side and keeping left of Lawns House.

At a T-junction bear right down to the valley road, then right again down to the entrance to Witherslack Hall.

> *Once a stately home of some eminence, it is now a special school for boys where yours truly used to be Head of Geography. Seen through the trees, this impressive edifice is reputed to be the home of a ghost appropriately named the White Lady who wanders the corridors at night.*
>
> *Resident staff who sleep in the attic section have reported strange noises coupled with cold draughts disturbing their slumbers. Could this be the spirited form of an old resident, or merely imagination and ancient walls playing their own cunning tricks?*

Continue down a track by the side of the school grounds, passing through a stile to cross the valley floor. Ahead lies the surging might of Whitbarrow Scar. Surely there can be few other limestone cliffs of such awesome and inspiring proportions as this in the north of England. On second thoughts, perhaps that at Malham Cove just tips the scales.

Whitbarrow Scar dominates the Witherslack Valley

Enter High Crag Wood over a ladder-stile bearing half right to follow the clear (frequently muddy after heavy rain) path snaking through the lower woods. This eventually merges with a bridleway that becomes a paved road serving Beck Head.

It is at this point that the Witherslack Beck debouches from the rock face. Just one of the intriguing peculiarities that personify the limestone bedrock. Only in the Yorkshire Dales have I come across this phenomenon on a more common scale. An interesting project would be to determine where the beck initially disappears.

Just before the road crosses the beck, take a right fork between two buildings to cross an irregular hotchpotch of gorse and bracken interspersed with trees. The path heads SSW to join a back lane. Head right along this to cross the main valley road dropping down past Birks Farm to a gate at the bottom. Lean half left across the field to follow the decaying limestone edge of Yewbarrow Scar.

After passing through a stile to reach Church Road head right for 100 yards, thence forking left past the small complex of High Fell End. Drop down through a gate to follow the hedge on your right down to another gate. We now enter the confines of Latterbarrow, a stretch of woodland preserved by Nature Heritage to combat the spread of unnatural development. Follow the clear path down to rejoin the original course of the A590.

A stream emerges from the limestone bedrock at Beck Head

A Bridge too Far

Devilish intrigue spans the thrashing waters of the River Lune

DISTANCE:	6 miles (9.7 km)
HEIGHT:	350 feet (107 m)
START/FINISH:	Plenty of parking is available in Kirkby Lonsdale near the Devil's Bridge on either side of the Lune
GRID REFERENCE:	616783
TERRAIN:	This mid section of the Lune Valley is characterised by a significant cutting in the limestone bedrock at KL with gently sloping foothills either side
NEAREST SHOPS:	Kirkby Lonsdale
USEFUL MAP:	OS Explorer OL2 Yorkshire Dales south & west

Prelude

Standing proud atop an elevated site within a bend of the River Lune, Kirkby Lonsdale has been a focal point for fairs and markets since its charter was awarded in the thirteenth century. So it might come as something of a shock that such a romantic setting has been linked with devilish intrigue.

Strung across the frenetic turbulence of the River Lune lies the awesome Devil's Bridge. This magnificent piece of arched stonework was built around the year 1365. The local vicar at the time was quick to spot a lucrative means of acquiring funds when he was granted the right of pontage *to collect tolls from travellers. Such monies were then used to maintain the structure which was the sole means of gaining the far bank until 1932 when the 'modern' bridge was built.*

Most visitors who venture across to the opposite side of the River Lune pause to admire the ancient pedigree of the bridge before partaking in some refreshment at the famed kiosk. It has become a mecca for motorcyclists at weekends and bank holidays. Few visitors, however, get further than the delightful environs of the shaded riverside. This walk attempts to remedy that omission by crossing little-used footpaths on the lower slopes of Casterton Fell.

But first a fiendish tale. The story is told of an old woman who arrived at the river crossing to fetch her cow for milking after it had strayed to the far side. Unfortunately by this time, the river was in full spate and impossible to cross.

At that very moment, the Devil appeared. "I will build you a new bridge," he said, "on condition that I take the soul of the first living thing to cross." The old woman agreed and returned home to await the morning. The Devil laboured all night and as dawn appeared on the following day, a magnificent new bridge spanned the foaming torrent.

Astonished at the Devil's accomplishment, the old woman was overjoyed and went to cross. Rubbing his hands at the prospect of a new recruit, Old Nick proclaimed with gleeful anticipation, "Now you must carry out your part of the bargain." "Certainly," announced the old woman hurling a small bun across to the far side of the bridge. "Fetch!" she called. Immediately, her dog ran across to retrieve the cake. "There," she exclaimed in triumph. "You can have the soul of my dog!"

As he fumed impotently at being cheated of his prey, the canny old dear crossed the bridge to collected her cow. With a howl of fury, the Devil threw himself from the bridge, leaving a handprint as a lasting memorial to his thwarted ambition, which can still be seen on the south side of the parapet.

The Walk

And so to the walk. Once you have crossed the bridge go over the A683 heading east up a lane and forking left up a narrow paved track. Climb steadily past a caravan site up to a junction. Take the hedged track called Laitha Lane heading north. Beyond the site, watch for a narrow wall-gap on the right.

Stroll up the field over a fence-stile until a ladder-stile is reached, allowing access to the field on the left. Climb over the crest and down to join a rough lane beyond. Lean right to reach the cluster of cottages at High Casterton. Head right along a lane then left, continuing east. Passing under the old railway bridge, bear right alongside it until a stile allows entry to a field.

Bear half left to meet a wall then up to cross the arrow-straight Roman road. Amble up the access track serving Bindloss Farm, keeping right

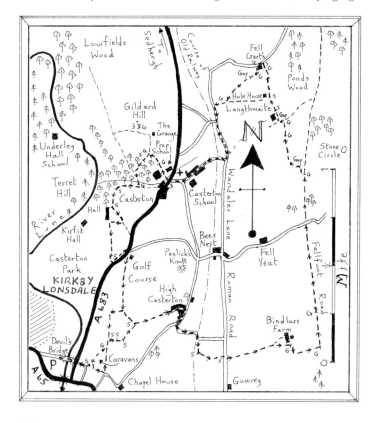

of the buildings. Go through a gate, bending right to reach a walled corridor that takes us up to the start of Fellside Road. Head north along this walled track running parallel to the valley at this mid point.

After crossing the Fell Road, watch for a gate on the left after 300 yards (274 m). Make a half right over to a wall-gap, bearing left to skirt a low knoll. The path drops down gradually to reach a track serving Langthwaite. Now take a left then a right to continue onward to reach the next farm, Hole House, and a wall-stile in the field corner.

Holy Trinity and the Casterton School, founded in 1820

Go past the tennis court to reach another crossing track. Enter a field and stroll over to Fell Garth where the back lane is joined. Following a short left, go through the gate at the far side of the farm to gain an open field. After passing through a gap in the fence, head south west down a long field to join the access road serving Hole House. Once on the back lane head south, bearing right at the second junction to arrive at Casterton with its fine towering church.

The village is dominated by the girls' senior school on this side of the main road, which we cross to locate a footpath that passes through the environs of the preparatory school buildings. The school was founded in 1820 by the Reverend Carus Wilson who became the incumbent of Holy Trinity Church, which was consecrated in 1833.

This gentleman gained his place in history as the founder of another school at nearby Cowan Bridge. The Brontë sisters attended this school which was set up for the daughters of clergymen. It became infamous as that portrayed so vividly in Charlotte's novel *Jane Eyre*.

Do not deviate from a straight course, passing through a gate that will bring you down to a reedy pool. Head left over a stile into a wood. The clear path fades near some broken branches. Keep right, avoiding

the steep ground ahead to reach a major track and a bridge. Head right here along the edge of the woods up to Casterton Hall.

The amended path circles left of the hall, continuing on the far side along a fenced corridor to join the main road. Bear left for 200 yards (183 m) to meet the start of Laitha Lane on the far side by the golf course. Head south, watching for a gate giving access over the caravan site. A stile deposits you on the narrow paved track to retrace your steps back to the Devil's Bridge.

The Devil's Bridge enjoys a colourful heritage

Laitha Lane is an old highway now used by walkers

All's Well at Shap

Harken back to a favourite Victorian health cure

DISTANCE:	5 miles (8 km)
HEIGHT:	450 feet (137 m)
START/FINISH:	Turn right off the A6 at Shap Lodge for the gradual descent to Shap Wells Hotel, parking on the grass verge just before the hotel entrance
GRID REFERENCE:	579096
TERRAIN:	Rolling bleak moorland to the east of Lakeland enclosed by numerous belts of coniferous forest
NEAREST SHOPS:	Shap
USEFUL MAP:	OS Explorer OL7 English Lakes south east

Prelude

Shap Wells Hotel is secreted in the shallow valley of Wasdale Beck close to its confluence with Birk Beck. This is not the renowned Lake District Wasdale revered by generations of climbers and hikers. Few people are aware of the valley's existence because there is little here to attract walkers who prefer rock beneath their boots. Here at Shap the Fells surrender to a more languid terrain.

The isolated situation of the hotel was no thoughtless endeavour. It was built in 1833 specifically for the well-heeled Victorian gentry. Owned by the Earl of Lonsdale, it became a fashionable resort due primarily to the healthy-giving properties of the nearby well. Adjacent to the main building is the old bath house, which was very popular with local nobility.

The waters are said to contain all manner of good things to invigorate the body, such as calcium, sodium chloride and epsom salts, the latter reputed to smell like rotten eggs. Dr Fife, an eminent Edinburgh chemist, said of the waters at the time that 'there is not a medicated spring in the kingdom more generally efficacious than the Shap spa, in raising the energies and inspiring the whole frame with a new animation and glow of health.'

Imbibing the waters in addition to bathing encouraged the prosperity of the hotel, which is still very much in business today. During the second world war, the building was commandeered as a POW camp for German officers, its most famous internee being the Nazi Rudolf Hess. After the war there was a period of decline until it was refurbished in 1962.

The Walk

Walk up the road to the left of the hotel complex, taking a track on the left just before a house. After passing through a stile, accompany a fence uphill that contains a dense stand of conifers.

> *The stone Monument is 23 feet high and surmounted by a sculpture of Britannia. Built in commemoration of Queen Victoria's accession to the throne, it was not erected until 1842 by the Earl of Lonsdale, William Lowther. Many of the carvings were done by Thomas Bland of Reagill near Shap.*

Go through a gap into the forest and follow a path that meanders down to a T-junction. Bear right here past the back of a house up to a gate. Beyond this, the path drops down to the Spa Well Head where visitors used to take a heated bath. All that remains today is stone capping beneath a canopy. The main path continues through the woods, soon crossing over to the right side of Blea Beck via a footbridge.

Climb up to the waterfalls where the path bends away right into a dark tunnel fashioned by close-set rhododendron bushes. This scary moment soon passes as a wall-gap is negotiated, followed soon after by a fence-stile. Now in the sepulchral quietude characteristic of coniferous forests, the path heads NNE in a straight line between the massed ranks.

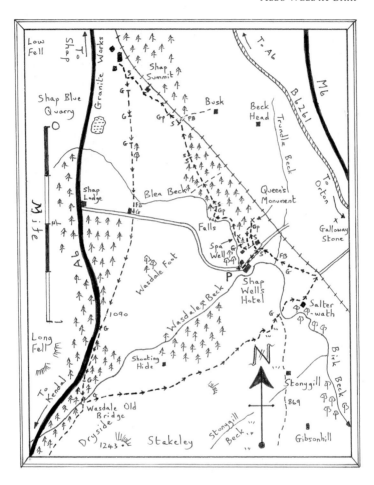

It crosses a forest road after 200 yards (183 m) maintaining the same course on the far side. Akin to a light at the end of a tunnel, the gloomy edge of the forest is reached after another 200 yards (183 m). Cross a wall-stile followed by a fence-stile to stroll along the outer edge of the

The Victoria Monument is hidden from view by conifers

Blea Beck provides a magnificent waterfall display

woods. Climb a shallow bank at the end to join the main north–south railway line.

Walk along this to mount a stile abutting the railway footbridge. Ignore a fence corridor leaning away to the left. Stick with the wall alongside the railway, passing through a fence gap after 100 yards (91 m). Drop down, continuing onward along a thin path to pass behind the house at Shap Summit. This is the highest point that the railway reaches.

Beyond the house, slant away from the railway to the left, locating a fence-stile close to the granite quarry operated by Cemex. Join the quarry track heading south and keeping straight ahead when it bends to the right.

Now a grass trail, this is the Great North Road used by Bonnie Prince Charlie in 1745 when he marched south endeavouring to reclaim the English throne for the Stuarts. After reaching Derby, he was forced to make an ignominious retreat, finally escaping back to France disguised as a woman, a story that has gone down in Scottish folklore.

Today this route has been superseded by the A6, the railway and the motorway and a vibrant imagination is required to conjure up the lie of the land in eighteenth century Cumberland.

After counting off three gates, you will have dropped down a shallow gradient to cross a field bridge spanning Blea Beck followed by another gate to cross the Shap Wells access road.

The green road continues beyond, climbing gradually to its highest point before another descent to the gate where the track merges with the main road for a quarter mile only. Another descent through a gate follows after which we cross Wasdale Beck by means of a substantial stone bridge with banks of conifers on either side.

On the far side, go through the gate on the left heading across bleak heather moorland. Ignore a grass path forking left that leads to a shooting box seen in the Wasdale Valley below. Our route drops down to an intake wall where, on my most recent visit, a distinctive intrusion akin to a giant matchstick poked from a cluster of stones. This is a Transco gas point. It would appear that even the most remote countryside is now subject to commercial interference. Nobody can halt progress.

Stick with the wall down into the valley until a farm bridge enables you to cross Birk Beck. Take the track past the farmstead of Salterwath until the railway bridge is reached. Then veer left, slanting away from the rising embankment and dropping down to pass through a wall-gate.

Lean half right to cross Trundle Beck via an ancient slabbed footbridge. The path beyond soon brings us to a stile giving onto the road opposite the entrance to the Queen's Monument. Bear left past the hotel back to the start.

The spa well once offered healing properties

Take the Bull by the Horns

Where the paranormal & pagan challenge established religion

DISTANCE	5.5 miles (8.6 km)
HEIGHT:	500 feet (152 m)
START/FINISH:	Park on the grass verge opposite the Methodist Church on the main street of Crosby Ravensworth
GRID REFERENCE:	621144
TERRAIN:	Featureless limestone moorland above the enclosed pastures of the Lyvennet Valley
NEAREST SHOPS:	Shap
USEFUL MAP:	OS Explorer OL5 English Lakes north east

Prelude

Barely reaching above the thousand-foot contour, the rolling fell country to the east of Shap harks back to the Dark Ages. Evidence abounds suggesting that these lonely moors were inhabited long before the Roman invasion. Cairns, stone circles, wells and the moss-coated footings of past settlements litter the undulating terrain.

Wandering across this bleak landscape, we are transported back into the mists of antiquity where life was a constant struggle to survive. Living in the cosy push-button world of the twenty-first century, it is difficult for us to imagine the harsh reality of existence for our Neolithic ancestors.

Crosby Ravensworth is on the route taken by these ancient tribes. An extension of the Roman High Street, it was pioneered more than four millennia ago. Once the Romans had departed in comparatively recent times, farming kingdoms ruled by princes emerged. They were of

Welsh origin and the area stretching from the Solway Firth, over to the Pennines and down into North Lancashire, became known as Rheged.

According to the Welsh poet Taliesin, one of the main rulers was a prince called Urien who lived at 'Lluyvened'. This Dark Age name has been passed down through the ages, continuing into the present day with the River Lyvennet. Here in its early stages, the beck is far less active than when it reaches King's Meaburn (see Walk 7).

A tributary of the Eden, this shallow vale enjoys a timeless appeal where little appears to have changed in centuries. The primeval elements on the moor to the west only serve to enhance the enigmatic quality of this lovely spot. No doubt one of the ancient settlements was the home of Urien and his family.

The Walk

Start off by heading north up the village street, slanting left by the Butchers Arms to cross the sub-tributary of Dalebanks Beck. Head left up the access road serving the Dale Head farms. After a quarter mile, fork right across a pathless grass slope aiming left of a stone barn ahead. Cross a plank footbridge spanning Blind Beck followed soon after by a fence-stile. Continue across the grass field, staying parallel with the road to pass through a wall-gate.

Join the access track for Harber but leave it when this clear route swings right. Drop down to slide through a narrow wall-gap. Keep below the farm buildings of Harber to locate another wall-gap-stile. A little further on, go through a wall-gate into the field above and along to another wall-gap-stile. After this, we slant down towards High Dalebanks, mounting a wall-stile en route. This is the end of the paved access road which we now join as a clear grass trail.

Beyond a gate, accompany this fine route in a steady uphill stroll. After two gates in quick succession, keep above the trees on your left. This route, complete with stone edgings, takes us all the way to the ancient farming hamlet of Oddendale. An enclosing curtain of trees was clearly planted to offer protection from the wind at this high altitude. The settlement just breaks the 1000-foot contour.

Head left along the top edge of the treeline where the path divides into three distinct arms. Our way should take the middle grass causeway heading south east. But first, take the right one for a distance of 328 yards (300 m). This will bring you to the Oddendale Stone Circle that lies offset on the right.

> It comprises two concentric circles of stones. The assumption is that Druids and others of similar belief used this for pagan religious ceremonies.

> But if perchance you experience a sickly, death-like smell and sense a 'presence' in the vicinity, you will not be the first to disturb the spirits that lie here. Others have witnessed the

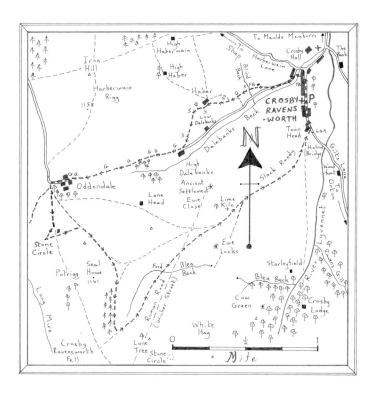

An ancient stone circle can be found near Oddendale

passing of a grey apparition across the moor which then disappears inside the circle. It has been suggested that this is due to the mound having been disturbed at some time in the past.

The most well known of these circles is that at Castlerigg above Keswick. Another of similar importance, though much less accessible is at Swinside, which will be visited by us during the course of Walk 31. Other earthworks and standing stones are also to be found along this ridge system stretching from Iron Hill in the north. Perhaps it was the bleakness of the terrain that stimulated the religious fervour of our ancient forebears.

Once you have communed with the whispering spirits of these primitive souls, head due east past an isolated building to locate the middle track where you swing to the right.

There is little across this bleak wilderness to break the monotonous regularity of the moorland swell. Lying just below the crest of the broad plateau, the view westward towards the Lakeland fells is restricted. That to the east encompasses the elongated stretch of the Pennines with the highest point of Cross Fell clearly visible. To its right, the weather station on Great Dun Fell presents the image of a giant golf ball.

The path is clear and will bring you to a line of conifers adjoining a walled enclosure. Amble between the upper wall and the line of trees to its end before turning sharp left. Accompany a thin track with the wall on your left, fording the upper reaches of Blea Beck after half a mile (800 m).

Soon after, we cross the direct line of the Roman road known as Wicker Street. Now indistinguishable from the surrounding rough pasture, it appears to terminate at an Iron Age settlement to the north called Ewe Close. Earthworks up to a metre in height are clearly visible and extend over a substantial area, indicating that this must have been a major settlement in the dim and distant past.

Thereafter, our route becomes sandwiched between converging walls, being channelled into the narrow gap of Slack Randy. Watch for a

This lime kiln is close to Ewe Lock

Crosby Hall conceals a strange secret

small circular earthwork 100 yards (91 m) off to the right of the track. Lower down is a lime kiln on the left close to an old limestone quarry. After this the grass path merges with a major field track.

Lower down it becomes metalled before joining the valley road at the southern edge of Crosby Ravensworth. Do not leave the village before visiting the magnificent church of St Lawrence at the top end. It dwarfs the small village and has been referred to as 'a cathedral in miniature'.

Close by is Crosby Hall. This plain and rather austere abode harbours a recalcitrant ghost of the most malicious persuasion. Reputed to have been the spirit of a former owner of the hall who was murdered, the spectre frequently took the form of a great white bull. The creature would slap and lick the windows with spiteful vigour, delighting in the fear engendered in the occupants, a farmer and his family.

Another of the ghost's wicked tricks was to shake the tower adjoining the main building until its bell chimed out a lusty chorus striking terror into the hearts of all the villagers. Such was the strength of fear generated by this odious spectre that in the early nineteenth century the tower was demolished.

Eventually, taking pity on the deranged farmer, the bull disclosed the location of a long-abandoned treasure trove. It also accurately predicted the fellow's final demise. So if the windows of Crosby Hall appear a trifle on the dirty side, blame should be laid squarely at the feet of the white bull, which was thereafter never seen again. This story has been saved for posterity by a local poet who recorded the tale in the local dialect thus:

> *Sometimes it lick'd window pane,*
> *In shape of a girt white bull,*
> *Sometimes it shak'd the mantle tower,*
> *Sometimes it towl'd the bell.*
> *And thus it carried on for years,*
> *To think on't maks yan whidder,*
> *Till 't auld man cock'd his head – an' then*
> *They beaythe went of f togidder.*

Woodland Wandering beside Windermere

Enjoy a monumental undertaking rewarded with stunning views

DISTANCE:	4.5 miles (7.2 km)
HEIGHT:	700 feet (213 m)
SUMMIT VISITED:	Latterbarrow 800 feet (244 m)
START/FINISH:	Ample pull-ins available close to the castellated entrance to the National Trust centre at Wray Castle
GRID REFERENCE:	371007
TERRAIN:	Tree-clad hummocks known as drumlins abound in the undulating arena to the west of Lake Windermere
NEAREST SHOPS:	Ambleside
USEFUL MAP:	OS Explorer OL7 English Lakes south east

Prelude

Approaching from the direction of Kendal, a prominent nodule pokes above the extensive forest covering on Claife Heights to the west of Windermere. This is Latterbarrow. A rather insignificant chunk of open fell, it offers a fabulous view across the lake to the high mountains behind, and as such it has been granted one of the most sturdy, rather than lofty, monuments in the whole of Lakeland. Reaching this noble edifice, though not its actual top, is an easy climb with more than enough encouragement to stimulate the optics. Enjoy it!

The stone ramparts that mark the entrance to Wray Castle give some idea of the architecture of the edifice itself. Enscosed within a sylvan screen less than half a mile (800m) to the north east, it is a neo-Gothic depiction of a medieval castle complete with battlements, buttressed towers and arrow-slit windows.

Some rather cynical commentators have labelled it a monstrous carbuncle that botches the natural beauty of the environment abutting Lake Windermere. Follies and artificial ruins are scattered around the grounds. The castle was built by a Doctor James Dawson from Liverpool with his wealthy wife's money. It is said that when the good lady arrived to view the finished building, her mouth dropped through the floor. Without faltering, she swept through the lower corridors and the back, never to set foot inside again.

Originally built as a private residence, it is not known how long the medic held onto the castle. Perhaps he welcomed the solitude it offered. Beatrix Potter is known to have stayed here with her family for their summer holidays.

The castle has passed through various phases over the years, becoming the headquarters of the Freshwater Biological Association and later being utilised as a training establishment for Merchant Navy radio officers. Today it is an Administrative Training College. The grounds are open to the public so judge for yourself as to whether or not Wray Castle is a blot on the landscape.

The Walk

Our walk begins by taking a track starting beside the stone church of St Margaret of Antioch.

Few visitors will be aware of this lady's place in church history. The saint herself dates back to the fourth century and has become something of a cult figure with over 250 other such church dedications dotted around the country.

This church was built in 1856 by Dr Dawson, whose tomb is located on the north side of the churchyard. Since 1954 it has been known as a chapel-of-ease, with services only held on special occasions, although Holy Communion is celebrated on a monthly basis.

Accompany the track with a wall on your left all the way down to the lake side at High Wray Bay. A tiny inlet, complete with its own

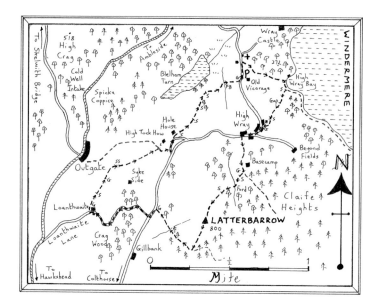

boathouse, makes for an idyllic sojourn. But not yet as we have only just set off. On the day I visited a pair of swans were in residence.

Continue round the shoreline to some woods. Before entering the thickly wooded confines at this northern limit of Claife Heights, go through a stile on the right. A gentle rise beside the wall on your right soon passes between a duo of stone posts. Lean to the left through another stile before circling right to gain the back lane at High Wray through a small walled gate.

Head left up the village street for 200 yards (183 m) taking a major track signposted to Basecamp. Beyond the entrance to this outdoor pursuits centre, pass through a side gate noting the vast array of locking devices used to secure the main gate (I counted seven).

The track then swings hard left into the dense covering of conifers. Watch for a thin path forking right and almost immediately mount a fence-stile. After stretching across a tricky ford, continue up a meandering path to the edge of the woodland. In this area, a great deal of coppicing has taken place in the past for charcoal production.

> *The original aim was to quickly replace the large amounts of charcoal needed in the days when the iron industry was rapidly depleting reserves of timber. Hazel is not a natural tree of the area and was imported specifically with coppicing in mind. Industrial exploitation was very much a feature of the Lakeland landscape in those days. Today we look on these activities as quaint and historic. But unfettered despoilation of England's green and pleasant land is clearly nothing new and can have devastating consequences for future generations.*

Mount a wall-stile and climb up onto the bracken-clad summit of Latterbarrow. Only to the south and east are the views restricted by extensive plantations of coniferous trees stretching away into the distance. Along the west bank of Windermere, Claife Heights has become well known for its plethora of nature trails. Perhaps less celebrated is the infamous legend surrounding the 'Crier of Claife'.

> *The Crier is said to have caused the drowning of numerous ferry passengers crossing the lake. Eventually locals refused to use the ferry service and business suffered accordingly. A monk was finally summoned to exorcise the recalcitrant boggle. This enigmatic spectre is now said to haunt an old quarry on the slopes*

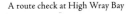

A route check at High Wray Bay

Few fell summits measure up to Latterbarrow

above Windermere where its spirit will be incarcerated until 'dryshod men walk on Winander and trot their ponies through solid crags.'

After marvelling at the prospect on offer, continue down the far side of the fell to the edge of the forest. Head sharp right along a thin trail with a wall and stream on the left. You will eventually reach a back lane. Bear left for 50 yards (46 m) then swing right along Loanthwaite Lane until you arrive at a farm of the same name.

Immediately beyond the farm building lean right through a gate following the hedge on your left. After mounting a stile, head for the gate at the far side of the next field. Maintaining a straight course you will arrive at a fence. Bear left to an unusual double enclosed stile with dog openings. (Any offers as to the purpose of this strange enclosure?)

From here take a north-east bearing, nudging the right edge of a wall to gain a field track close to High Tock How. Mount a stile on the right, thereafter swinging left then right to gain a narrow access lane. Make a left at this point, continuing ahead when the metalled lane leans right. After passing Hole House, mount a stile accompanying a grooved track along to another. You will then drop down to a hidden stile in a hedge adjacent to a small wood.

Follow the hedge on your right around over the next stile past the broad expanse of Blelham Tarn. Lean left away from the hedge past a clutch of trees to cross a stone footbridge. Then keep right alongside a fence to reach the High Wray lane soon after. A left past the Old Vicarage will return you to the church access track.

Savour the Flavour of Ripe Fruit

Perhaps sandwiched twixt green slices of Winster & Gilpin

DISTANCE:	5.5 miles (8.6 km)
HEIGHT:	650 feet (198 m)
START/FINISH:	Half a mile (800 m) beyond Winster village en route to Bowness, take a right fork off the A5074 and park on the grass verge adjoining a narrow crossroads
GRID REFERENCE:	14944
TERRAIN:	Scattered clusters of trees are interspersed with small tarns amidst this subdued landscape
NEAREST SHOPS:	Bowness-on-Windermere
USEFUL MAP:	OS Explorer OL7 English Lakes south east

Prelude

Less than two miles from the pounding heart of Lakeland can be found a rolling landscape of which few people are aware. No surging peaks here. No deeply scoured valleys to quicken the heartbeat. Here is to be found a rather unobtrusive amalgam of scattered woodlands and narrow lanes where it is extremely easy to lose one's sense of direction.

There is a distinct absence of notable landmarks. A glance at the map of this area to the east of Lake Windermere presents a chaotic splay of features that are impossible to analyse. It is as if some giant sculptor, having finished his work in the centre, has gathered up all his residue and throw it down here.

And therein lies the area's inherent fascination. It is possible to criss-cross the twin valleys of the Gilpin and Winster in this one simple walk with only a modest amount of upward perambulation, none of it too steep. Paths criss-cross the terrain, swinging between stands of trees and small exposed clusters of rock.

And with very few people encountered, here we are presented with an idyllic throwback to a gentler, slower epoch. Within a short distance is the bustling metropolis of Windermere.

Winster village is a scattered collection of settlements which this walk circumvents. The heart would appear to be located on an old cross-roads with the Brown Horse Inn dominating the scene. Farming has always been king, the knotty nature of the terrain pointing to sheep and cattle pasturing.

The Walk

We begin our travels at an old crossroads from which we head east along Green Lane. When the paved section terminates after a quarter mile, continue ahead along this rough-walled track that climbs gradually across the hummocky crest before dropping down through a wood. The walls are coated with a thick carpet of green moss, which in springtime contrasts with the brilliant gold displayed by large clumps of gorse.

A much-favoured time to visit this locality is late summer when the damson crop is coming to fruition. Then again, early Spring can be another splendid time, when exuberant white damson blossom bursts forth from the bud. Dazzling white petals of the damson trees give the appearance of a rogue snowfall in mid April, and, many farmers claim that the eighteenth is the best time for seeing the blossom at its best.

The wooded limestone fells provide a welcome screen to shelter the fruit-bearing trees from storms blasting in from across Morecambe Bay. Limestone is said to imbue a certain sweetness to the soil, which has helped to establish the area as a special place for damson cultivation in Britain. In the past, some farms have been known to produce over fifty tons of fruit in a season. These days, unfortunately, they would be lucky to reach five in view of declining tree regeneration.

On reaching the road, head right for 200 yards (183 m) then left at the first junction to drop down into the Gilpin Valley, named after Richard de Gylpin who hailed from Normandy in France. For his boaring exploits, see Walk 17. When the road leans sharply to the left, continue ahead on a narrow highway that is little more than a track.

Just beyond Thornyfields, go through a gate to make a steady ascent back over towards Winster. With a wall on your left and the steep tree-lined flank of Bow Mabble Breast on the right, pass through another gate before reaching the crest of the ridge. The clear track descends the far side beyond a wall-stile.

Emerging onto the main valley road below, cross straight over through a gate. Drop down, keeping right to locate a hidden gate. Straddle a narrow rill by a slabbed footbridge to join Crag Lane. Passing through

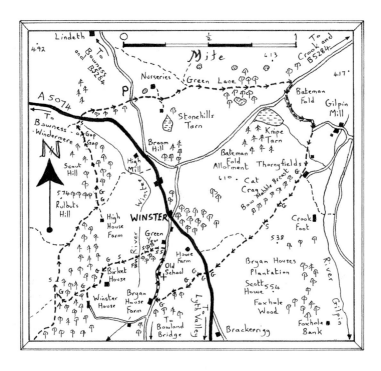

133

The original Holy Trinity church had a steeple

a gate, the grassy track crests a low rise, soon joining a back lane through a gate opposite Bryan House Farm. Head right along here to pass Holy Trinity Church.

> The first church on this site dates back to the seventeenth century. It included a stone steeple that cannot have been well built because in 1692 it fell down. Some of the debris landed on a parishioner called Ann Compston who was shocked but fortunately not harmed by the startling occurrence. This lady resided at what is now the village post office, built in 1600.

A far more robust steeple was then erected similar to that of St Anthony's at Cartmel Fell (see Walk 13). The church was completely rebuilt in 1875 but needed alterations in 1929 to accommodate a new organ. Continue heading north down the road past the nearby Old School House. Dating back to 1849, it closed its doors to pupils in 1902. Today it acts as a meeting hall.

After a quarter of a mile (402 m), watch out for a signpost pointing the way west just before Green Yew. Mount a stile and another soon after to enter a small wood. Emerge at the far side over another stile then keep to the left side of the trees to locate a stile and footbridge spanning the River Winster.

The name Winster is thought to have come from the Norse vinstri, meaning left, as opposed to the Gilpin Valley, which is to the right. Another theory stems from the discovery of white clay in the river bed which has led to claims that Winster has to be the white stream.

Climb up the far side with a wall on your right. A stile and two gates will find you joining a major track that heads left to arrive at Winster House. Bear right beside this substantial slate house to pass through a gate into a narrow walled corridor. This climbs steadily uphill through the trees, emerging above into the open through a gate.

Here we join a clear track heading right across a broad plateau. Lying between the deeply entrenched Lake Windermere and the Winster Valley, the views over the Lake District heartland are spectacular. The lake remains hidden within the glacial trough at all times. Descending in a gradual manner the track reaches a gate in less than a mile. Here, we slant left alongside the wall to pass through a narrow wedge of trees gated at each side.

Now heading north, stick with this clear path through scattered clusters of trees, passing through two wall-gaps. Then make an abrupt swing to the right along a walled passage to rejoin the main valley road. Opposite is the rough start of Green Lane which we follow back to the crossroads from where we started.

The school house closed its doors in 1902

Visit the Brown Horse at Winster after the walk

135

Forcing the Issue

Follow the path of a murderer from Skelwith Bridge

DISTANCE:	6 miles (9.7 km)
HEIGHT:	650 feet (198 m)
START/FINISH:	Immediately after crossing Skelwith Bridge on the busy A593 bound for Coniston, a pull-in for three cars is available on the left. Alternatively, park on the Langdale road adjacent to the hotel
GRID REFERENCE:	345033
TERRAIN:	Lumpy countryside associated with a glacial landscape is interspersed with hard rock where ice action has resulted in cascades of breath-taking proportions
NEAREST SHOPS:	Ambleside
USEFUL MAP:	OS Explorer OL7 English Lakes south east

Prelude

Skelwith Bridge has long been a favourite stopping point on the road to Coniston or Langdale on account of its waterfalls, not to mention the refreshment offered by the hotel. Being close to the road, both are easily accessible. Try to leave the hotel's attractions until after you have finished the walk.

The cascades make for impressive viewing, especially after heavy rain. Hidden behind the later addition of the hotel and enclosed within a steeply wooded gorge, the waterfalls were original raison d'etre of the Skelwith hamlet a source of power for bobbin mills. Another major activity was the dressing of slate quarried in the valley.

Behind the dominating Skelwith Bridge Hotel, are to be found numerous slate cottages, beside which a splendid gorge thunders past.

The thrashing waters of the River Brathay 'force' their way eastwards through the narrow ravine to swell Lake Windermere close to Clappersgate.

The hotel lies at a major fork in the highway for those heading down Great Langdale or onwards to Coniston. Many a noggin can your guide recall in the bar during his youth whilst staying at the nearby Neaum Crag. The steep climb back up to the campsite soon dispersed any after effects.

The Walk

Walk up the road towards Coniston for 200 yards (183 m) keeping well into the right verge as there is no footway. Two thirds of this walk follows the 70-mile (113 km) long-distance footpath known as the Cumbria Way. It stretches from Ulverston, heading north through the heart of Lakeland to finish at Carlisle. We leave it at High Park then rejoin it at Elterwater for the walk back to Skelwith Bridge in the opposite direction to that normally taken.

Fork right along the second right-of-way to accompany a clear path that winds gradually uphill. After emerging from the tree cover through a stile, merge with the access track serving Park House. Still heading in a westerly direction, the next settlement passed is Park Farm.

It should be noted at this point that this route is infamous for a particularly heinous murder that occurred some two centuries past. A certain Betty Briggs had been attending a weekly function at Clappersgate with her beau, Jack Slype, who harboured designs that were not to the young lady's taste.

To his chagrin, she chose to dance with a gardener who then offered to escort her back to Tilberthwaite at the end of the evening. The spurned suitor followed them all the way back to Oxenfell Gate where he killed the gardener. Realising the gravity of the act, Jack Slype immediately took his own life. From that moment onward, the macabre rumour spread that each night the shape of a ghostly figure walks this route. An after-hours wander is therefore not recommended for the fainthearted!

After the next dwelling at Low Park, the path enters a constricted passage stiled at each end, before dropping down a steeply wooded banking to gain the Elterwater road close to Colwith Bridge. Enter the woods on the opposite side following the River Brathay round to Colwith Force.

Do not venture too close to the abrupt downfall as there will be little chance of you completing this walk or any others should you tumble into the swirling maelstrom. The path then veers away from the river, climbing gradually to exit the closely packed woods above. Stroll alongside a wall to pass through the farmyard of High Park.

Once on the road, head west for a quarter of a mile (402 m) until Stang End is reached. Bear right just beyond the farmhouse down a walled track to cross a footbridge spanning the Brathay. On the far side climb a thin pathway to gain the Little Langdale road near a cottage.

Head left for no more than 50 yards (46 m) then lean right past the buildings of Wilson Place. After passing through a gate, climb a clear trail that will bring you to the old road connecting Little Langdale and Elterwater. Hang a right along this rough walled lane up to the first gate.

Immediately beyond this strike up left through the trees on a path that carries you over the valley crest to descend the far side into Great Langdale. After crossing an old miners' track, stroll down to the metalled road serving Baysbrown. Bear right past a cottage then left through the quarry yard.

This is one of the few working quarries remaining in the District, so care should be exercised when negotiating the concourse. After rounding a building watch for the path forking left down past the rising spoil tips to meet the beck below. Here we rejoin the Cumbria Way. The path accompanies this watercourse round to the right downstream to Elterwater. As well as being a quarry village, in its heyday Elterwater utilised local ash charcoal to make gunpowder used for the quarry blasting.

Leave the Little Langdale road at Wilson Place

After crossing the stone bridge, slant immediately right past the car park and through a gate to stroll along the side of the river as it debouches into Elterwater itself. Probably the least known of the lakes, this is due in no small part to its irregular shape, and reedy nature. This path provides the only public access to its shoreline.

Elterwater is much smaller than it used to be following the passage of the ice sheet down Great Langdale. This is due to significant in-filling that has taken place. No doubt the lake will disappear in due course, like the one that occupied the upper end of the valley beyond Chapel Stile. Glimpses of the elusive lake can be snatched through the tree-cover as you follow the clear track back towards Skelwith Bridge.

The path closes with the valley road passing through a gate at the point where the river is squeezed into a tumbling gorge at Skelwith Force. Passing through the slate-finishing yard, we stroll behind the new hotel before reaching Skelwith Bridge itself and the termination of a fine low-level traverse of mid-Langdale.

Slate is still quarried in Great Langdale

The Britannia at Elterwater is on the Cumbria Way

140

First Aid for the Tewets
Keeping in step with St John

DISTANCE:	7.5 miles (12 km)
HEIGHT:	750 feet (229 m)
SUMMIT VISITED:	High Rigg 1163 feet (354 m)
START/FINISH:	Make use of the car park and picnic site located 300 yards (274 m) north of Legburthwaite Church on the left of the B5322. Or a small pull-in for two cars 300 yards further on
GRID REFERENCE:	318195
NEAREST SHOPS:	Keswick
TERRAIN:	Rough fell country along the ridge followed by flat valley pastures on the return
USEFUL MAP:	OS Explorer OL4 English Lakes north west

Prelude

Three essential elements uppermost in the minds of all fell wanderers relate to ruggedness, height and a shapely appearance, not necessarily in that order. I am sure you will all have your own favourites that meet these essential criteria. I feel equally certain that High Rigg will not be amongst the chosen few.

Such an omission does not mean this diminutive eminence is unworthy of exploration. Far from it. What it lacks in altitude is more than made up for in craggy outcroppings scattered around the perimeter. And you are guaranteed one of the finest low-level ridge walks in the Lake District.

The northern prospect across to Skiddaw and Blencathra is second to none with a stunning reverse view down Thirlmere a wonderful added bonus. And all without the crowds that invariably frequent more famous destinations. It was the ascent of High Rigg that first prompted my wife Ann to set herself the arduous and daunting challenge of conquering Scafell Pike. A feat she duly accomplished later that particular year with her customary style and aplomb.

The most popular highway through central Lakeland nudges the western slopes of High Rigg, yet rarely will a glance be offered to this crusty fell.

And to the east, the secluded Vale of St John provides a shortcut to the A66 but sees little stopping traffic.

The Walk

Starting from the car park, turn left to reach the A591, swinging right over Smaithwaite Bridge. Mount the ladder-stile then fork left off the low-level red herring to ascend the open wooded slopes at the southern limit of Naddle Fell. This is the steepest part of the climb which will eventually find you skirting the upper reaches of Wren Crag.

Looking back across the narrow valley, the precipitous slab of Castle Rock is clearly in view. It has been romanticised in Sir Walter Scott's poem The Bridal of Triermain. *He selected it as the principal scene where in*

> *'… the midmost of the vale, a mound arose,*
> *with airy turrets crown'd,*
>
> *Buttress and rampire's circling bound, and mighty*
> *keep and tower...'*

The awesome north face with its severe overhang was only conquered in 1939 by Jim Birkett, a quarryman from Little Langdale. He was one of the pioneers of rock climbing in the Lake District. The Rock has also acquired a reputation for being haunted. Climbers have experienced sinister forces within its environs, no doubt inspired by its resemblance to a Gothic castle of horror.

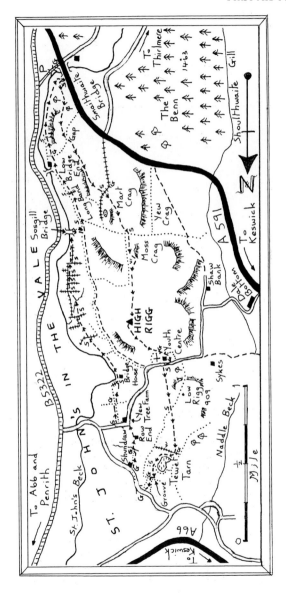

Mighty Skiddaw peeps over the shoulder of lowly High Rigg

Keep to the St John's side for an exhilarating stroll along the crest after passing through a wall-gap concealed in a depression. Once a fence-stile is crossed, the path wanders over to the opposite side of the ridge skirting the splintered ramparts of Mart Crag. Drop down to straddle a wall that divides the fell.

From here accompany a clear green sward on the left of the wall towards the summit of Naddle Fell, known as High Rigg. Only slightly higher than competing outcrops, the rocky summit is easily recognisable, with its neat cairn perched on a crag table.

On a clear day, our objective of Tewet Tarn twinkles merrily in the sunlight. All around, the breathtaking array of mountain peaks vying for attention is awesome. A steep descent on short grass will soon find you at the small pass where the Church of St John and the Catholic youth centre repose. Take some time out to rest awhile in the idyllic setting of this remote house of God. Festooned with daffodils in spring, few graveyards can be so inviting.

As its name implies, the church is dedicated to the renowned Hospitallers of Jerusalem whose descendants now administer first aid. Buried here is John Richardson, a nineteenth-century dialect poet of some renown. He was born at nearby Piper House and taught at Bridge House close to the church. He died in 1886. Richardson's work can be difficult for outsiders to understand but he talked about life in the vale as locals experienced it and in their own tongue.

At this point you need to decide whether to continue onward or take the shortcut back around the lower reaches of the fell. If the latter course is chosen, walk down the road past the church taking an obvious track that forks right. This clear track will lead you back to the main road.

Those who opt for the extended walk should take note of a signpost opposite the church. This points the way over the easy grass slope of Low Rigg. After mounting a wall-stile, drop down to go through a gated fence close to what on closer inspection is a somewhat reedy tarn.

On a calm day, the profiles of north Lakeland's premier giants are reflected in the placid waters. It is apparent that this lower section of the ridge is much less defined. Circle around the right side of the tarn to mount a wall-stile. Soon after, an unusual groove in the rock strata

St John's church is dedicated to the founders of First Aid

Castle Rock towers over St Johns-in-the-Vale

145

is followed right down to a wall-gap where a track winds down to the road below.

Turn right for a quarter of a mile (402 m) for the return journey. Leave the road, keeping right of Shundraw and continuing ahead through two gates. With a wall on your left, watch for a small gate which allows access to the opposite field. Descend a flight of stone steps, crossing to a slate bridge over the narrow stream before continuing onward towards Row End, soon after reaching a lane opposite Yew Tree Farm.

Take a left then right through a gate into the field behind. Keeping the wall on your right, amble along to mount a stile, swapping to the far side of the wall through a gap. A short walk will bring you to John Richardson's old schoolhouse close to the banks of St John's Beck. Follow it round to pass through a wall-gap, after which slant away half right over to a fence-stile. A stream is crossed halfway across the next field by a footbridge.

Join a fence and accompany it up to another fence-stile. Same thing again as you make a half-left traverse of the next field with a foot-bridge midway. Here we join a grooved grassy lane with a fence on the left. Stick with this and straddle a number of stiles until you finally reach Sosgill Bridge. This is a superb example of an old packhorse bridge that is still in use.

Swing right here towards the towering ramparts of High Rigg to join the clear track skirting the eastern edge of the fell close to a barn. Head left over a stile, sticking with this track and skirting round Low Bridge End Farm where refreshments can be had.

The clearly defined path meanders along a varied course before mounting the precipitous lower wooded slopes of Wren Crag to round the promontory at the entrance to the vale. After mounting the ladder-stile onto the main road, bear left retracing your steps back to the car park.

In Step with the Cistercians
Monastic habits take priority at Cartmel

DISTANCE:	6.5 miles (10.5 km)
HEIGHT:	300 feet (91 m)
START/FINISH:	If parking is not available adjacent to Cartmel Priory, make use of the race course car park on the western fringe of the village for which a small charge is made
TERRAIN:	Extensive woodland cloaking the gently shelving western slopes of the Eea Valley on a limestone base
NEAREST SHOPS:	Cartmel
USEFUL MAP:	OS Explorer OL7 English Lakes south east
WARNING:	This walk should not be attempted during race meetings. The final section which makes use of a right-of-way traversing the course will be closed for obvious reasons

Prelude

This wander around Cartmel makes for a fine walk at any time of year. When approaching the village from any direction, St Mary's Priory cannot fail to impress even the most incredulous visitor. Solid and unyielding, an irrepressible legacy of early Christian endeavour, the monks were known as 'black canons' on account of their dark cloaks.

The order pursued an elaborate ritual of daily observances enclosed within the grounds of the priory. Only on very special occasions were they allowed to vacate the premises. The Cistercian Way which forms part of this walk indicates one particular route they followed.

Arriving here in the twelfth century, the first canons proceeded to lay the foundations for a new church on what was felt to be the most fitting situation. Where else but on a local hill. This became known as Saint Bernard's Hill. It was only later, following a visionary experience from on high, that the site of the current church was selected.

The off-set belfry was added in the fifteenth century, both for economic reasons and to limit the strain imposed on supporting pillars. Its stalwart individuality was hailed by Millom poet Norman Nicholson. He once attempted to write a poem about the priory but only managed the first line before giving up. It began 'God's box of bricks'…

At the end of the walk, if time permits, I strongly recommend that you visit the interior of the priory. Stone walls and a flagged floor lend an air of antiquity to this ancient pile. One particular curiosity is to be found in the north-east corner of the nave where a shelf is located containing a loaf of bread.

This was initiated at the bequest of local resident Rowland Briggs who died in 1703, leaving funds for the bread to feed needy householders of the parish. A brass plaque narrates this philanthropic action that was much appreciated at the time. Today it acts as a quirky reminder of modern society's profligacy.

The Walk

Begin by heading south west along a cobbled route known as the Cistercian Way. Beyond the isolated Seven Acres, we enter Lane Park Woods. The track kinks to the right in the middle before exiting. Soon thereafter it becomes paved and splits. Take the left arm for half a mile (800 m) until you are opposite Low Bank Side. Then mount a stile on the right to climb through the woods. Mount a wall-stile at the top end to walk along the right side of a wall to a corner stile. Another 100 yards (91 m) and we rejoin the Cistercian Way.

Bear right alongside a wood, which on my last visit bore the cogent warning that adders are in the vicinity. After half a mile (800 m) at the edge of Yaw Yeat Wood, take a clear left through a gate to follow the walled section of the Cumbria Coastal Way up to the next gate. At the end of the walled corridor, keep right to reach a wall. Soon after

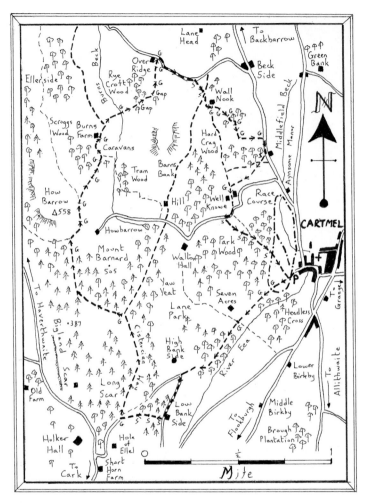

passing through a fenced gate, fork right across broken ground to reach the caravan site at Burns Farm.

Swing right by the farm buildings through a gate heading in a north-easterly direction. After crossing Burns Beck and through another gate,

Cartmel Priory dominates the narrow village streets

St. Bernards Mount hovers above the Cistercian Way

the indistinct trail goes through an open cluster of trees. Beyond a wall-gap, we swing away to the left and a second wall-gap, aiming for Over Ridge and a back lane. Head right down here for a quarter of a mile (402 m) until a gap-stile in the hedge on your right is located. Make a diagonal crossing of the field to gain the access road serving Wall Nook.

Head right to pass this old farm, now a modern business centre. Keep right of the buildings to mount a grass slope passing through two gates to reach an open field. Aim for the midpoint of the woods on the far side. A fenced passage through here, gated at each end, will bring you into a field.

Customary loaves from the bequest of Rowland Briggs

Cross to a small gate on the far side slanting left down the right-hand side of a hedge to reach the road below. Lean right towards Cartmel for 200 yards only (183 m). Opposite Garret House mount a stile in the hedge on your right. Make a half-left crossing of the field cutting straight across a paved track. After nudging the edge of a wall ahead, lean half right up a slight gradient to reach a major track through a gate.

From here bear left past Well Knowe to arrive at a back lane serving Howbarrow only. Bear right for 150 yards (137 m) before mounting a stile on the left. Follow the left edge of a field to enter Park Wood through a gap-stile.

Stroll down to the lower edge of the woods to cross the race course heading south east back to the car park.

151

A Shelter For Roffe

Where the cross of Jesus was held by a brave hero

DISTANCE:	6.5 miles (10.5 km)
HEIGHT:	550 feet (168 m)
START/FINISH:	Park on the main street of Hutton Roof keeping well in to the right side
GRID REFERENCE:	571783
NEAREST SHOPS:	Burton-in-Kendal
TERRAIN:	A shallow valley of rolling hills and pasture between limestone uplands
USEFUL MAP:	OS Explorer OL7 English Lakes south east

Prelude

Try to locate the name of Hutton Roof in any guide book to the north of England and you will extremely hard pressed. Although well known locally, it lies off the main routes so is rarely visited. Only those specifically wishing to make the acquaintance of this remote settlement are likely to drive along the single street.

Located on the spring line below the sheltering bulk of the craggy upthrust that some might figure gave the village its name, Hutton Roof was once a major farming community. It dates from the twelfth century and probably relates to a certain Roffe who built his huts around here.

The small church was built in 1881 and is another designed by Lancaster architects Austin and Paley (see Barbon – Walk 34) who described it as 'a good honest job'. Inside there is a memorial to the Reverend Hardy who officiated here before, as the famous hymn says, he became a Christian soldier marching as to war, where he was killed. His gallantry was recognised by George V who gave him the ultimate accolade of a posthumous Victory Cross. A tablet in Carlisle Cathedral also asks of this brave man, 'What is courage but the inspiration of the spirit?'

Sandwiched between the bold upsurge of Hutton Roof's limestone crags and the undulating foothills to the east lies the Lupton Valley. Unknown and untrammelled, it offers fine rambling terrain for those who prefer their own company. Along the excellent network of footpaths, you are guaranteed a degree of seclusion rarely found in our crowded island.

The Walk

The walk begins at Hutton Roof by taking the walled track at the north end of the village that heads west up onto the crags. After passing through the gate adjacent to Linden Lea, bear left through the bracken to visit an unusual perched boulder. Naturally I cannot encourage walkers to scramble onto its vegetated top, even if the view affords a magnificent prospect over Hutton Roof.

Keep plodding up the clear trail, passing through the lyrically titled Blasterfoot Gap. On the left is to be found one of the finest examples of limestone scarring and angled pavement in the district. The path then crosses the northern edge of Hutton Roof Crags on the highest part of the walk. Pause awhile to scan the rustic beauty of the vista over the remote Lupton Valley.

Continuing onward, the path snakes through a cluster of gnarled juniper trees before finally joining the fell road in the gap between Farlton Knott and Hutton Roof Crags. Head right, taking the minor road with its central grass line until a sharp left turn is reached by a lone house. Go through the gate opposite to make a diagonal crossing of the field.

After the gate in the corner, head left beside a hedge to join a back lane via a stile. Head right then immediately left towards Lupton. After 20 yards (18 m), a hedged track forks right. Accompany this all the way round to another lane at Badger Gate. On your left is Lupton Beck, ensconced in a surprisingly steep-sided ravine.

Bear left down a lane for 100 yards (91 m) before leaning right through a gate to cross rough ground below Badger Gate Farm. Parallel Lupton Beck to strike up a shallow rise through a fence gate and aim towards a hedge stile. Beyond, a patch of reeds known as the Rabbit Warren

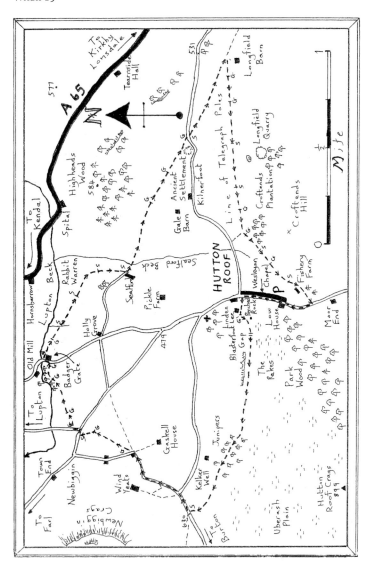

Investigate the perched boulder overlooking Hutton Roof

(all bunnies must have been in hibernation when I passed this way) is traversed to the top corner.

Mount a stile to accompany a fence for 150 yards (137 m). Then make a wide right-hand swing around a hillock to reach the access road serving Sealford. Veer left along a hedged track heading south east. The first gate brings you into an open grass sward. Keep onward through the next gate to reach a back lane.

> *Close by on the right is the site of a primeval settlement, the outer ramparts of which can still be picked out. Could this have been where Roffe first settled before moving to the site of the present village?*

Cross the lane to straddle a stile, maintaining a straight line nudging a limestone wall after 200 yards (183 m). With this on your left amble along this right-of-way from a pre-historic era, squeezing through two gap-stiles adjoining gates. Opposite the crumbling ruins of Longfield

Trace the foundations of this early settlement   A tiny chapel for a big hero

Barn below on the right, cut back, now heading west passing through a fence gate as you descend the grass pasture into a dry valley.

From here the footpath aims arrow-straight to Hutton Roof, not visible on the far side of the Longfield hill. Even in mist it is impossible to get lost on this section due to the chaperoning presence of a line of telegraph poles. After passing through a gate in the valley bottom, a sharp pull is needed to reach the wall-stile at the top end of the field.

Straddle the grassy crest to begin the descent into Sealford Vale, still accompanied by the ubiquitous poles. In the late afternoon sun, the old strip-field farming system stretching down to the beck from Hutton Roof is revealed, harking back to a period long since consigned to history.

At the bottom bear left through a short but overgrown section of woodland stiled at each end. Accompany Sealford Beck along past Fishery Farm to gain the road south of Roffe's 'huts'.

How's this for a Tarn?

Opposites attract when crag & tarn shake hands

DISTANCE:	6 miles (9.7 km)
HEIGHT:	750 feet (229 m)
SUMMIT VISITED:	Black Crag 1056 feet (322 m)
START/FINISH:	Tom Gill car park just south of Yew Tree Tarn on the main road between Anibleside and Coniston
GRID REFERENCE:	322999
TERRAIN:	A rugged lower-lying landscape cut by deep valleys heavily wooded with tarn-filled depressions
NEAREST SHOPS:	Coniston
USEFUL MAP:	OS Explorer OL7, English Lakes south east

Prelude

Surprisingly, although of modest height, Black Crag offers one of the finest viewpoints in central Lakeland. Only when the summit trig. column is reached can the true majesty of the delectable panorama be truly appreciated and enjoyed.

Few people are likely to have even heard the name of the fell, which is hardly surprising as it barely creeps above the thousand-foot contour. Displaying all the attributes of a fell accorded the distinguished honour of mountain status, Black Crag will not disappoint.

This walk also provides the opportunity to stroll along the shoreline of Lakeland's most popular tarn whilst venturing into rarely travelled upland scenery of the highest quality. Every step of the way is a joy to behold. Choose a midweek out-of-season day to avoid the inevitable encounters with others of the human race around Tarn Hows. If you are lucky, you will have the walk to yourself.

The Walk

Our wanderings begin with a steep ascent up the left side of Tom Gill. Accompany this turbulent creek up a meandering track, climbing above the array of splendid waterfalls amidst the tree cover to emerge onto the west shore of the Tarns.

Although the most-well known beauty spot in Lakeland, Tarn Hows should not be disparaged in any way. It is a fine expanse of water, secluded and unseen within a shallow hollow ensconced by a wooded necklace.

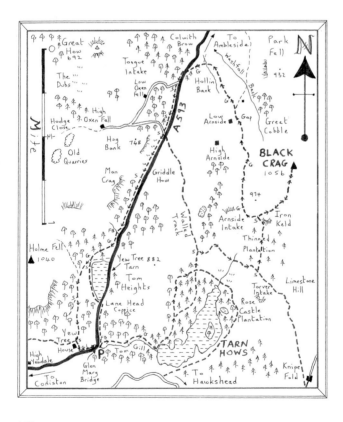

Originally consisting of three separate tarns, dams were built to merge them into a single reach by James Marshall of Monk Coniston Hall. It was he who planted the spruce and larch conifers that now surround the tarn. Beatrix Potter bought the area in 1930 for the express purpose of securing it for the National Trust.

One story is told of a Troutbeck giant by the name of Girt Will who lived in a hut on the edge of the tarns during the Middle Ages. Many people were afraid of him, but he proved to be a good worker and became accepted. However, Will could not resist a pretty face and kidnapped a local beauty. After being pursued by her betrothed, both of them were drowned in the swirling waters of Yewdale Beck.

Even today Tarn Hows is a place that all solitary fell wanderers should visit once in their careers. The overexposure will certainly rekindle one's appreciation of the more lonely outposts in the District. Therein lies the appeal of this particular walk.

One incident always sticks in my mind when visiting Tarn Hows and harks back to the days before global warming. This was when winters were really cold and seemed to go on forever. I well recall taking a shortcut across the tarn, not in a boat, nor on the back of a passing trout.

It was December of 1961 and the tarn froze over, much to the delight of skaters who skimmed effortlessly across the glistening ice, a weak sun glinting off their shiny blades. Doubtless these days the over-anxious safety denizens of officialdom would have all manner of no-access signs prominently displayed.

William Wordsworth likewise relished the experience of winter sports back in the early nineteenth century, which he elucidated in The Prelude *thus:*

> *'… All shod with steel,*
> *We hissed along the polished ice in games*
> *Confederate, imitative of the chase.'*

Slant left along a wide track that soon forks away from the water's edge. At a junction where the path divides, take the upper arm into

Savour the tranquil ambience of Tarn Hows

the surrounding woodland. The path drops down to a major cross-roads which is signposted. Straight ahead lies the main trail around the tarn.

Our route breaks sharp left soon, emerging from the tree cover as it heads north to join a rough walled lane. This once formed an important link between Hawkshead and Langdale and gives some idea of the type of route common in the District in the early days. Climbing gradually for half a mile (800 m), watch for a stile on the left giving access to the recently thinned conifer plantation of Iron Keld. The Forestry Management Agency is keen to promote the natural recovery of the undergrowth, which conifer planting has all but destroyed.

The path now heads north, still climbing steadily until we arrive at the next stile in a solid fell wall. Take a right from here to follow a thin yet clear path over a cluster of rocky outliers which are also part of Iron Keld. Thereafter, the scabrous plinth of Black Crag can be seen ahead to the north across the treeless expanse of Arnside plantation area.

Black Crag offers a stunning view over Windermere

A short pull will deposit you on this noble edifice which boasts a National Trust plaque. And it is testament to the fell's pre-eminent situation that Scafell Pike can be seen eight miles distant on a west-north-westerly bearing. Having partaken of the delights afforded from this lordly vista, return to the main fell track at Iron Keld and head right.

Soon passing through a wall-gate, make a leisurely descent going through another gate to reach the isolated farm of Low Arnside. Just beyond the wall-gap near a small hut up on the right, watch for an indistinct fork angling left. Drop down to a wall-corner to slip through another gate.

Follow the wall on your right all the way down a grass bank, circling round to the left through a small cluster of trees to join the main Coniston road. Head left, crossing over to join the path that parallels the road. Cross over the Oxen Fell access road, down which is located Oxenfell Gate where Jack Slype jealously terminated the life of his rival (see Walk 26). Continue along the path that accompanies the main road towards Coniston on the right side of a wall.

We stick with this all the way down a gentle gradient to reach Yew Tree Tarn. The path soon leans away from the road through open woodland until a gate is reached in the intake wall. Accompany the path on the far side, heading south below the surging ramparts of Holme Fell. Straddle a fence-stile, continuing due south up to a sharp right-hander.

Mount the ladder-stile on the left to walk down a walled track joining the main road by Yew Tree House with its celebrated weaving gallery. In recent times it has become even more well known in movie circles as the home of Beatrix Potter. A short stroll towards Ambleside will return you to the car park.

Yew Tree House with its spinning gallery

Circling Round the Fells
Step back into prehistory to commune with Neolithic man

DISTANCE:	7 miles (11.2 km)
HEIGHT:	750 feet (229 m)
START/FINISH:	Turn left off the A595 just before the Millom road into the village of Hallthwaites. Ample roadside parking is available near the Church of St Anne
GRID REFERENCE:	178855
TERRAIN:	Deep valleys score the high fell country to the north offering easy access to the lonely moors that characterise this south-west corner of Lakeland
NEAREST SHOPS:	The Green
USEFUL MAP:	OS Explorer OL6 English Lakes south west

Prelude

Few people will be aware of the Whicham Valley, sandwiched between Millom Park and the mighty bulwark of Black Combe. Of glacial origin, being straight with steep sides and a flat floor, it forms the extreme south-west boundary of Lakeland. Tiny farming settlements abound in this area, Hallthwaites lying in the valley of Black Beck. A rippling wedge of upland divides the two main valleys that have their origins deep within the heartland of Swinside Fell.

It is the prehistoric stone circle close to Swinside Farm that is our objective on this foray. Enigmatic and obscure, primitive and arcane: all words that could describe the aura of mystery that hangs over these strange yet compelling relics of Bronze Age man.

Of the seventeen known circles in Lakeland, the most famous is that at Castlerigg near Keswick. It receives at least a thousand visitors to every one that makes the trek to Swinside. Tucked away on a lonely moor hemmed in by the rolling hills behind Black Combe, very little is known of Swinside's raison d'etre.

All of these primeval artefacts, especially the stone circles, present a fascinating conundrum that still baffles all who seek to delve into their obscure past. Meeting places, certainly. But whether for pagan religious ceremonies in the pre-Christian epoch is pure speculation. Being the earliest physical features of our ancestors that have survived is both fascinating and perplexing.

The Walk

Our walk begins near the new church of St Anne at Hallthwaites. Of nineteenth-century origin, it replaced an old chapel down in the valley where the grey hamlet in the hollow is located. Begin by walking back up the A595 towards Broughton for 328 yards (300 m) turning left along a signposted track. At the corner of the field, accompany the wall round to the right up to a gate.

Then slant left and right again to enter a walled corridor. This opens out beyond a stile before resuming as the track drops down to the woods abutting Whicham Beck. Here the beck is squeezed into a narrow cutting by the surging prow of Knott Hill on the right and Greystones opposite.

Pass through a gate close to the ruins of Knottend as the track bears right across the lower flank of Knott Hill. Initially following a walled passage, then a wall on the left, the track soon veers away right. When it fades, aim for the mid point of the wall ahead to locate a gate. Thereafter the path strengthens, passing through two stiles to cross the bleak expanse of Knott Moor.

The upper reaches of Whicham Beck lean away to the left and its origin by Stoupdale Crags. The stone circle is now in view immediately ahead to the north. Head straight for it, joining a fell track which is the main access for Swinside Farm 200 yards (183 m) beyond the

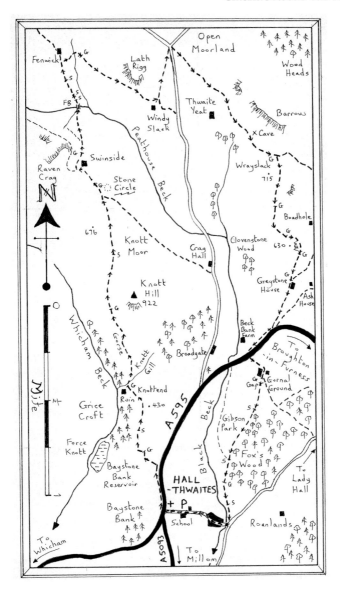

Knott Hill is the highest point in the area

circle. A gate allows access to the monument, which over the eons appears to have remained relatively in tact.

> *It is a puzzling phenomenon in an age when Britain is bursting at the seams with too many people that this small corner stays remote and rarely visited. Yet in past millennia, there must have been many more people residing in the vicinity for such a major feature to have been constructed.*

Continue up the track to pass left of Swinside Farm, continuing on the far side around the lower edge of Raven Crag. When the main track begins to rise, fork away right along a series of grooves. Aim down into the cutting occupied by Peathouse Beck, crossing it by a substantial footbridge close to where a minor stream converges. Ascend the slope on the far side mounting three stiles to reach Fenwick.

Bear right before the farmyard along a clear track that swings right through a gate to head down the far side of the valley in a south-easterly direction. At a sharp kink adjacent to Windy Slack, head left into a shallow ravine. Keep heading due north to climb gradually onto the open moor soon arriving at a road junction.

Take the grooved track that heads south west, keeping to the top side of Black Beck and passing Thwaite Yeat which is on your right. After 300 yards (274 m) watch for a flooded cave in the rocky slope on the left. Stick close to the wall on your right until a gate is reached. Our route now heads south around the slopes of Wrayslack, passing over grass pasture through three gates before the steep descent to Graystone House.

Join the access track to reach the main A595. Head right for a quarter of a mile (402 m) until a rough track on the left can be taken. Wander down this, swinging right through the yard of Gornal Ground. Avoid the obvious walled track heading downhill beyond the gate. Take the field track through a gate followed soon after by a gap. Keep ahead through another gap with a fence on your right. Stroll across rising ground then down to merge with the upper edge of Fox's Wood on the left.

Straddle two stiles as you drop down to the lower wood to enter a narrow passage. Maintain a southerly course from here, eventually strolling along the bank of Black Beck and joining a back lane by a bridge. Head right through the village of Hallthwaites up the hill back to the church.

Swinside Farm huddles below Raven Crag

Swinside stone circle

A Green Quarter of Kentmere

Where a giant amongst men raised his game to a new level

DISTANCE:	8.5 miles (13.7 km)
HEIGHT:	1000 feet (305 m)
START/FINISH:	200 yards (183 m) beyond the access track over the River Kent is a pull-in on the right at the start of this walk. It is sufficient only for two cars. Another lies just before the works entrance
GRID REFERENCE:	456015
TERRAIN:	A gently shelving plateau above the steep sided glacial moulding of Kentmere
NEAREST SHOPS:	Staveley
USEFUL MAP:	OS Explorer OL7 English Lakes south east

Prelude

Kentmere is a valley of contrasts. The upper section is rugged and brutal, displaying a fearsome countenance that cannot be ignored. Here the effects of glacial erosion on the landscape are truly awesome. Ice-ravaged peaks stand proud and aloof overlooking the deep valley head. Kentmere village lies on the distinct separation of the hard volcanic rocks from the more yielding Silurian slates down valley.

For centuries upland passes on either side of the valley on the dividing line have provided easy lines of communication between the parallel valleys. Referred to as Sleddale Forest, the appendage is a misnomer as all the original trees have been cleared from this bleak plateau.

Only on the lower sheltered slopes have coniferous plantations emerged, and they are only small and insignificant. This featureless wilderness has little to offer the hard rock enthusiast who has eyes only for the craggy upsurge to the north. An easy-going system of tracks crosses the area, making it ideal for those who prefer to have the fells to themselves.

The Walk

Pass through the gate at the edge of a small cluster of trees to climb the valley side. Another gate after 50 yards (46 m) finds you ascending a stony track with tree cover on either side. Once this initial steepness is completed, the rest is easy.

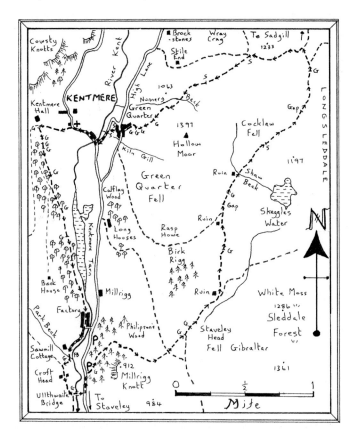

The clear track forges through endless tracts of dense bracken, soon passing through another walled gate. Merging with a straight-walled enclosure and accompanying it for 200 yards (183 m), we arrive at a crossing of bridleways. Continue ahead, striding through a duo of walled gates. The track now veers away from the wall, forking close to an old ruin.

Take the left branch to pass through another gate, climbing steadily to reach another junction with a large old hut on the left – one of many such features littering the plateau. Half a mile (800 m) to the right the bleak expanse of Skeggles Water can be seen in a shallow depression. Keep heading on a north-easterly course to gain the highest point of the walk on Cocklaw Hill.

Thereafter we drop down through a wall-gap swinging north to gain the main link route between Kentmere and Sadgill in Longsleddale. A stiff climb left will find you cresting the pass. Slip through a stile on the left to accompany a thin trail across the northern slopes of Hollow Moor down to the farming hamlet of Green Quarter.

This old ruin is past near Skeggles Water

St Cuthbert's is a plain but solid house of God

Three gates and a zigzag will deposit you on a paved access road. Stroll down to the main core of this odd little enclave of stone dwellings. Right of the sharp road bend, take a stile to descend a grassy bank into the woods below, and so down to another narrow lane. Bear left then right to gain the centre of Kentmere village adjacent to the austere church of St Cuthbert. Fork left along the access track serving Kentmere Hall on the far side of the valley.

> *The original robustly defensive pele tower abuts a more recent farmhouse that was added once the dangers from invading brigands had passed. This ancient pile has witnessed many strange happenings during its checkered history, but none is so quirky as that involving Hugh Hird who was known as the 'Cork Lad of Kentmere'. Employed by the De Gilpins on account of his enormous strength, it was Hugh who single-handedly lifted the thirty-foot kitchen beam into position after several local lads had struggled in vain to complete the awesome task.*

171

Kentmere Hall beside the sturdy old pele tower

Summoned to attend the court of King Edward in London, the giant endeared himself to the Crown by performing spectacular feats of strength. His mammoth appetite was no less impressive. A whole sheep washed down with copious flagons of wine was a mere snack to the 'Cork Lad'. Hugh spent the rest of his life in the Troutbeck Valley moving colossal boulders and uprooting trees. It was this latter exertion that finally sent the enormous fellow to meet his maker.

A working farm, Kentmere Hall affords an engaging link with a turbulent past that has no equal in today's Lakeland. From here the path

172

makes a U-turn in front of the hall to head south at valley level. Immediately beyond the second gate, cross Hall Gill on a footbridge. After entering Hall Wood, watch for a fork in the clear trail. Take the left arm to follow the lower trail to the air filtration works.

Kentmere Tarn is much smaller than when Hugh Hird passed this way. Described in 1577 as 'a poole a myle compass', it was drained around 1850 to deliver more land for pasturage and cultivation. The extensive reed beds give some indication of its original dimensions. Two ancient dugouts and a Viking spear were found, offering evidence of much earlier settlement in the valley.

At the far side of the works, stroll up the paved lane to Sawmill Cottage where a fenced passage traverses the private garden enabling you to reach the far side. Straddle a footbridge over Park Beck, leaning right through a gate. Saunter up a walled corridor to reach a major fell track. Head left past two substantial houses, taking a left to cross the River Kent by Ullthwaite Bridge. Back on the valley road, another left for a quarter of a mile (402 m) will return you to the start.

Another Lunar Exploration
A Gaunt view of Gilbert's order

DISTANCE:	6.5 miles (10.5 km)
HEIGHT:	1200 feet (366 m)
SUMMIT VISITED:	Green Bell: 1984 feet (605 m)
START/FINISH:	Approaching from Tebay, turn right off the A685 for Ravenstonedale and park at the junction of the first side road on the right
GRID REFERENCE:	716044
NEAREST SHOPS:	Ravenstonedale
TERRAIN:	Once the intake fields are left behind, all is open grass moorland rolling across upland fells
USEFUL MAP:	OS Explorer OL19 Howgill Fells and Upper Eden

Prelude

Pronounced Razendl, the ancient village of Ravenstonedale has become more enticing for the discerning walker since being circumvented by a rapid-transit link route over the Pennine watershed. This bypass effectively discourages any thought of dalliance by passing motorists. Once again the village can settle back into the beguiling remoteness it once enjoyed as a matter of course.

Perhaps it was this seclusion that encouraged the Gilbertine Order of monks to settle here back in the Dark Ages. In those far off days at the start of the last millennium, the order comprising both men and women chose this location to build a priory, the foundations of which can still be seen adjoining the present church of St Oswald's.

An unusual sect with their own laws and customs, the Gilbertines are the only true British monastic order, all the others having originated on mainland Europe. Indeed they came across the Pennines from the east coast in Lincolnshire where St Gilbert drew a small group around him in 1089. The sect finally arrived in Ravenstonedale where they adopted the down-to-earth approach to life for which they were revered.

The church has an interesting stained-glass window on the east side in memory of Elizabeth Gaunt, the last woman to be burned at the stake in 1685 for her non-conformist beliefs. Noted for benevolent works, the good lady was accused of harbouring traitors by one of those whom she had sheltered. This cowardly action was due to the fact that the blackguard had learned that anybody who gave evidence would be pardoned for their crimes.

Another unusual custom, practised until its final demise in 1623, was the right of sanctuary. Any criminal who entered the portals of the church and managed to toll the bell would not face any charges, no matter how scandalous the transgression.

It is little wonder that fugitives from all over the north came to Ravenstonedale to gain an easy remission of their sins. With felons who had committed bloody murder being released back into the community without a stain on their heinous character, it is not surprising that James I decided that something had to be done. And so ended the right of sanctuary.

There was also a court held in the church that became known as 'The Peculiar Court of Ravenstonedale'. It was commissioned with the task of implementing the total authority of law within the manor, a duty which was exerted in full measure atop Gallows Hill on the far side of the main road and now known as Park Hill.

The Walk

Make your way up the road that serves Greenside Farm for 100 yards (91 m), then head right through a gate and alongside the wall on your left. Keep with this field track into the next field after which you will arrive at a walled corridor gated at one end only. Cross the next field until a disintegrating barn is reached.

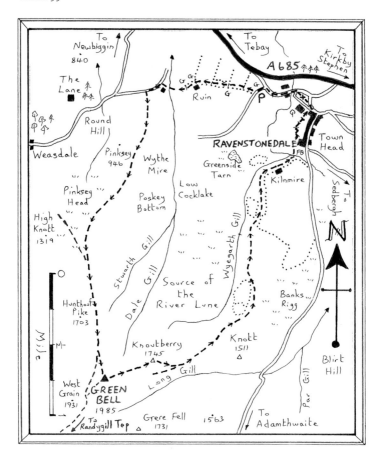

Pass through a gate changing to the opposite side of the wall. Another gate gives onto a track which drops down to cross Greenside Beck, thereafter keeping right of an old house to gain a metalled farm road. Now bear left until the accompanying wall veers away to the right. Where the road enters open country slant left along a tractor track keeping left around the marshy depression of Tailor Mire.

You may be fortunate enough to witness fell ponies roaming these moors. But should you be unlucky enough to break a leg, don't expect these noble creatures to offer assistance!

Indistinct initially, the track heads SSW across the grass flank of Pinksey ,becoming more pronounced as height is gained. Continue due south up a gradual incline past the lone-cairned outpost known as Hunthoof Pike – a clear reference to its equine residents. Just beyond here, leave the direct trail to fork left up a newer addition that will bring you to the summit of Green Bell. This is one of only three in the Howgills that boast a trig column.

The highest peak in the vicinity is Randygill Top a mile to the south west which exceeds the magical 2000-foot contour by 47 feet. Green Bell just fails to meet this requirement for mountain status by a thick whisker. If you cannot resist the temptation to include a 'mountain' in the day's itinerary, a simple path links the two summits and adds two miles to the distance walked.

From Green Bell, head north east down a gently sloping ridge past a sheepfold on the left. These slopes mark the spring where Dale Gill emerges, together with the headwaters of the mighty River Lune. One

Fell ponies wander freely over the Howgill Fells

Examine the remains of the old Gilbertine priory

of the north's premiere watercourses, it swings west at Newbiggin eventually making a dignified exit beyond Lancaster at Sunderland Point, a distance of 70 miles. Streams to the east of Knoutberry, soon reached up a brief rise, feed into Scandal Beck and the River Eden.

From the top of Knoutberry, drop down pathless grass slopes to the south east, aiming for an obvious path on the far side of the Long Gill valley. Accompany this down under the shadow of Knott, keeping to the right of a walled enclosure. Continue heading due north to reach the first of the intake walls, after which the track strengthens on the approach to the outer 'suburbs' of Ravenstonedale on the right bank of Wyegarth Gill.

Join the second span of a double footbridge ascending a grassy, walled lane that opens out in an area of rough grass. Keep with the stony track up to a metalled lane, turning left then immediately right along this one for 100 yards (91 m). Watch for a stile on the left enabling you to cross to the opposite corner of a small walled pasture.

Straddle another stile into a vegetable allotment, the right-of-way being a grass path between the lettuce and cabbage patches – at least it was when I last came this way! At the far side enter an open field and cross straight over to a gated stile at the opposite side where dense woods are entered. A thin trod cleaves a way through the undergrowth down to a fence-stile.

Over this, walk down through the trees to an access lane, following it round to the right then left to gain the main street. Bear left past a secondhand book dealers to fork right past the village school and enter the churchyard through a gate. At the far side of St Oswald's can be found the excavated remains of the old priory.

Continue to the far side of the church yard and out of the gate to cross an open grass tract to another gate at the far side. This brings us out near to the Kings Head where a left will see you strolling back along the old road to the starting point. While ambling down the lane, keep an eye open for the ravens that gave the village its name. In the eighteenth century, their capture was rewarded at the rate of two old pence per head.

Pottering over the Fells

Natural architecture combines effortlessly with that of St Bartholomew

DISTANCE:	9 miles (14.5 km)
SUMMIT:	Brownthwaite 1433 feet (437 m)
HEIGHT:	1150 feet (351 m)
START/FINISH:	Park by the parish church in Barbon
GRID REFERENCE:	631825
TERRAIN:	The rolling moorland upthrust on the east side of the Lune Valley is split by the deep cutting of Barbondale
NEAREST SHOPS:	Barbon
USEFUL MAP:	OS Explorer OL2 Yorkshire Dales south & west

Prelude

There is a swift link between Kirkby Lonsdale and Sedbergh by way of the main A683 through the Lune Valley. On any weekend, beware of over-powered motor bikes roaring along this relatively direct route, where serious accidents are not unknown.

Yet only half a mile (800 m) to the east at the mouth of a deep gash in the valley side lies Barbon. A quiet and unassuming village, it has given its name to the link with Dentdale and the Yorkshire Dales, known as Barbondale. In the centre, at what was once an important route focus, lies an ancient preaching cross close to the Barbon Inn, which began life as a stop-off for the mail coaches.

The church of St Bartholomew is on the site of a much earlier chapel dating from 1610. The present church, designed by Lancaster architects Paley and Austin, was consecrated in 1893 by Lady Shuttleworth at a cost of £3500. When asked whether the east window should be of stained glass she replied, 'The view from this window cannot be improved by man and should stand as a frame to the glory of creation.' And who are we to disagree?

The original stonework and huge oak beams imbue the building with an aura of strength and permanence, and this lovely church is well worth going into.

The first vicar was the Reverend James Harrison who installed the four bells and the tower clock, not to mention the fine lychgate dated 1915. This church is one of the seven Rainbow Churches that belong to the parish of Kirkby Lonsdale, the others being at Kirkby Lonsdale, Lupton, Hutton Roof, Casterton, Middleton and Mansergh.

The Walk

Take the road beyond the church on the left that serves Barbon Hall. After crossing Barbon Beck it swings right uphill. Fork right off the access road after half a mile (800 m), entering the woods through a gate to chaperone the beck. Perhaps it was in the prattling beck hereabouts that the beaver, introduced by Norse settlers, once thrived, giving the name Barbon to posterity.

A clear track forges upstream emerging from the woods by another gate at the end. Keep onward above the beck to pass through the final gate before reaching the open fell. Another 100 yards (91 m) will bring you to a footbridge. Stroll back towards Barbon for a quarter mile.

Just beyond Blind Beck Bridge, take a clear path striking left up the fell side. Opposite a waterfall, the path cuts back on an abrupt zigzag to join the original bridleway. Continue up the easy gradient, eventually arriving at a gate giving onto a walled corridor down to Bullpot Farm.

This remote dwelling has given its name to a nearby pot hole lyrically referred to as Bull Pot of the Witches, a favourite of local potholers. It was the last farm in the district to be freed from the ravages of the snow blizzards of 1947. The resident sheep dog was an old guy of fourteen years named Hemp and this brave hound was responsible for rescuing upwards of one hundred sheep from the drifts, some of which had been incarcerated for several weeks living on their fat supplies.

Our way lies along the fell road which rises briefly prior to the steep descent into Casterton. We leave it at the first bend through a gate on the right. The fell track circles round the upper edge of Gale Beck climbing steadily up to a wall. Leave it here accompanying the wall for a quarter of a mile (402 m) to the highest point of the fell known as Brownthwaite.

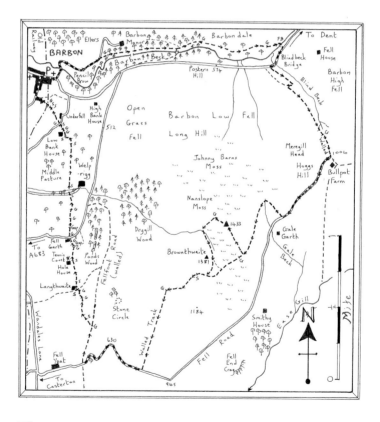

Architectural excellence at Barbon

An extensive view opens out across the bleak expanse of Lower Barbon Fell to the north and Middleton Fell on the far side of Barbondale. Leave the trig column, aiming for a gate due west at the wall-corner. Keep to the continuing wall until a grass path emerges on the far side of a ditch.

Follow this left past the stony eminence on the right. Take the right fork when the path divides to rejoin the original fell track. After mounting a fence-stile, the path joins another wall to reach a walled track leading directly down to the fell road. Bear right down this steep highway and just after the second sharp kink, take the track heading right.

This is an old walled connecting track known as Fellfoot Road. Running in a north and south direction, it parallels the course of the Roman road that made use of the Lune Valley two thousand years ago. After three hundred metres, go through a gate on the left, crossing diagonally to a wall-gap. Immediately swing left, following the wall around through two more gates to reach a track adjacent to Langthwaite.

Bear left to continue through a gap and stile to reach Hole House. Keep left of the tennis court across a grass patch to cross another

Bullpot Farm is now a potholing clubhouse

Cross to the far side of Barbon Beck

track. Make your way across the facing field to cross straight over a back lane near Fell Garth. Keep heading north over the next four fields to reach the wooded access road serving Whelprigg, one of the largest houses in the area.

Stiled at either side, make your way across Middle Pasture, which is dotted with an intermittent collection of ash and oak trees. At the far left corner mount a wall-stile bearing left towards Low Bank House. Pass through a gap-stile to continue past the farm, followed by a narrow fenced passage to reach another back lane.

Make a half left through the gate on the far side eventually crossing the old railway where the right-of-way goes through a private garden. Amble down a narrow lane turning right at the bottom to enter Barbon past the post office and village store.

A Spring in your Step
Beware the ghost of a notorious highwayman

DISTANCE:	6 miles (9.7)
SUMMIT:	Wansfell Pike: 1597 feet (487 m)
HEIGHT:	1250 feet (381 m)
START/FINISH:	Make use of a small car park after turning left off the A592 just before the Jesus Church at Troutbeck
GRID REFERENCE:	412028
TERRAIN:	Clear paths all the way in fine upland scenery that is typically Lakeland
NEAREST SHOPS:	Troutbeck
USEFUL MAP:	OS Explorer OL6 English Lakes south east

Prelude

Most visitors to this part of Cumbria will be aware of the village of Troutbeck, yet still it remains an enigma. Hidden away from prying eyes, this tranquil oasis has to be positively sought out. The only car park is down near the main road opposite the old school house. There follows a pull up narrow paths to reach the single main street. Many visitors are thus only able to afford it a passing glance as they drive through. Comprising an array of period cottages, the most famous is Town End a quarter of a mile (402 m) south of the village proper. It is well worth a visit, as it does remain virtually unchanged. It was the home of the Browne family who lived there for over 300 years from 1623.

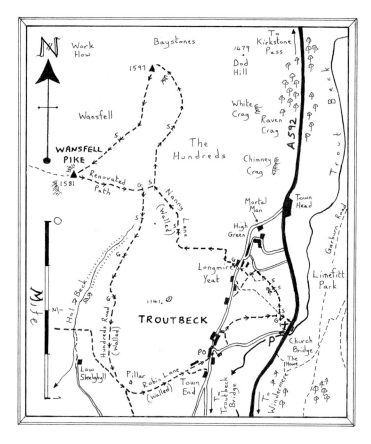

The Walk

Our walk begins by passing the slate-built Jesus Church (see Walk 15). Take the first left after the church up a rough walled lane. Watch for a stile on the right after 100 yards (91 m). A clear path points the way over the lower fields. Mount a pair of closely situated stiles continuing onward to a crossroads. Make a left along a track then right up a constricted and hedged pathway that climbs up to the main street of Troutbeck.

The scattered nature of the village means it is linked by an array of inter-connecting paths. Bear left for no more than 50 yards (46 m) then take the track branching right through a gate. Climb away from the village up a twisting walled track across a gently shelving fell known as the Troutbeck Hundreds. This soon becomes a straight thoroughfare.

> *On a hot June day in 1953, it suffered one of the worst down-pours in living memory. Trees were snatched out by the roots, walls disintegrated. With calamitous effect a deluge swept downhill, flooding the village and washing away the road.*

At a distinct bend, the main path to Wansfell Pike branches left through a wall-stile. Our route continues up Nanny Lane until a ladder-stile is reached on the left. Cross to the far side of the wall accompanying a thin trail that parallels the wall as far as an arrow painted onto a rock. Follow the direction left to mount the fellside, soon gaining the elongated ridge.

A fine cairn adorns this lesser known end of Wansfell that is slightly more elevated than the main top that can be seen a mile (1.6 km) distant to the south west. The switch-backed path follows the ridge mounting a wall-stile midway. The main summit and most popular with visitors from Ambleside boasts a well-worn plinth surmounted by an untidy cairn. It offers a superb prospect across the upper reaches of Windermere to the mountains beyond.

Leaving here, a path much renovated and re-laid winds down the rock-encrusted fellside. Before reaching Nanny Lane, we pass through

Pause for reflection on Wansfell Pike

Enjoy the peaceful ambience of Troutbeck

a wall-stile then swing immediately right following a series of guide posts over the grass sward of the Hundreds. Beyond a wall-gate, continue straight ahead over rolling cropped grass pasture ignoring the clear track that forks away to the right. We soon drop down to meet a gravel track known as Hundreds Road.

This soon becomes walled, merging with the track ascending from Ambleside. These tracks offer a far more realistic idea of how travel in previous centuries really was. This walled thoroughfare is now known as Robin Lane, very apt for a highway that once served as the back entrance to Low Skelghyll, from where a wily cove by the name of Monkswell planned the robberies that made him a much-feared predator.

Assisted by a gang of cutthroats, he preyed upon wealthy travellers in these sparsely populated dales. This mysterious scoundrel remained a thorn in the side of what law existed for many years until his arrogance got the better of him. Only by accident was the infamous career of Monkswell brought to an untimely conclusion. Having been engaged in some degenerate intent, the gang returned to Low Skelghyll late one night.

Unfortunately for them, one of the servants had become suspicious of the strange comings and goings at the house. He waited until all was quiet before investigating the stable, there to discover lathered horses covered in mud from a hard ride.

But most damning of all, on the floor lay a highwayman's mask. Monkswell realised his error the next day. Aware that the game was up, he disappeared with his entire gang. What became of the cunning brigand was witnessed firsthand exactly a year later by a local squire.

Sir Michael Fleming of Rydal went to the trial of a certain Monkswell at the Old Bailey in London. Discovering it was his one-time house guest, Sir Michael related how the sly miscreant was convicted of pursuing his old trade down south. A one-way trip to the hangman at Tyburn Tree brought his notorious career to an abrupt termination.

Low Skelghyll is hidden from view further down the slope on a tributary of Hol Beck. Our route now descends gradually to the southern end of Troutbeck village. Arriving at the post office, take a walk along the single main street which comprises an array of stone cottages and farms. These have grown up along a line of wells from which the communal water was once obtained, many of which were named after saints.

After 100 yards (91 m) bear right down to a paved square known as High Fold. A track heads north descending the fenced lower pastures until a gate is reached. Cross a narrow stream beyond to rejoin our outward route. At the bottom, as an alternative, pass though the gate on your right, returning to the main road through the churchyard.

In the Pink
A wander around the remotest tarn in Lakeland

DISTANCE:	5.5 miles (8.6 km)
HEIGHT:	1450 feet (442 m)
START/FINISH:	On the road over Birker Fell between Ulpha and Eskdale, park down the right turn serving High Ground. It is opposite the access road serving Devoke Water
GRID REFERENCE:	171977
TERRAIN:	A ring of crusty fells surrounds the upland hollow occupied by Devoke Water
NEAREST SHOPS:	Eskdale Green
USEFUL MAP:	OS Explorer OL6 English Lakes south west

Prelude

Awesome, inspiring, momentous, exhilarating — adjectives by the bucketful slip effortlessly off the tongue. If for no other reason, the fells surrounding Devoke Water should be climbed for the spectacular eastern prospect they afford.

From the summit of any single one, the scalloped horizon is all encompassing. Such noble leviathans as Scafell, Bow Fell, Esk Pike, Crinkle Crags, Pillar, not to mention the roof of England, Scafell Pike, jostle each other to hold centre stage.

Satisfyingly remote and inspirational in fine weather, it quickly becomes a bleak and inhospitable wilderness to trap the unwary when mist descends to cloak the fells in a cloying embrace. In such conditions this is no place for the novice walker. Leave it for a sunny, or at least clear day. The celebrated artist William Heaton Cooper remarked that no other tarn in Lakeland reminded him more of the Scottish Highlands than Devoke Water.

Few other views will have your lower jaw trailing on the ground. But beware. Paths are faint and frequently disappear altogether. The hazards of becoming lost beneath a dank mantle of the grey stuff, sentenced to wander for all eternity across the lonely moors, cannot be taken lightly.

So remote is this locality that persecuted Quakers established a community at Woodend which lies half a mile (800m) south east of the tarn. The hamlet had its own school and became self-sufficient, far removed from any interference. The bodies of deceased members of the group were buried close to the tarn in softer ground. They are identified by small simple headstones characteristic of this austere sect.

The Walk

Stroll up the clear track from the fell road heading in a south-westerly direction. You will soon encounter one of those strange anomalies that often crop up in the fell country, namely a lone gate in good condition attached to nothing. Pass round the side and continue along the track until the shimmering reach of Devoke Water appears.

At this point branch right across rough grassland, aiming towards the cluster of stones rising behind the north bank of the tarn. Make a wide left-hand sweep to gain the rocky promontory, picking a thin path in the grass towards the latter stages.

Rough Crag, together with its neighbour Water Crag (which is our next port of call), is on the southern limits of the Eskdale Granites. Examination of the rocks on the summit will reveal the distinctive hard pink rock. Forming a line of weakness at the junction of the Borrowdale Volcanic rocks, a glacial depression was created that is now occupied by Devoke Water. As we shall see, the fells to the south are of a completely different rock type.

A clear path points the way over to Water Crag half a mile (800m) to the south west across a shallow dip in the ground. Man's colonisation of the land to the south and west dates back thousands of years to the Stone Age. Apart from numerous cairns, of which hundreds have been found dating back to

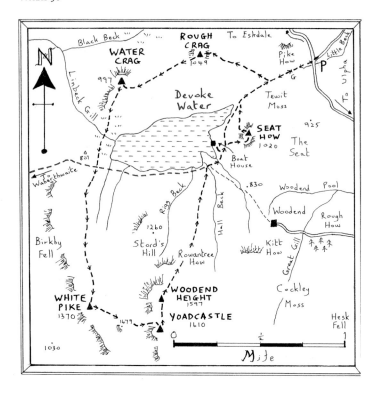

the Bronze Age, nothing remains to indicate the presence of human settlement. Yet bronze age farmers were assiduous in their clearance of the forested tract that covered the land hereabouts.

In consequence, much of the soil was eventually washed away to leave an impoverished landscape. Archaeologists have uncovered evidence that crops were grown around the shores of Devoke Water, where a thriving settlement existed some 2000 years ago. The only dwelling of any note that remains is Woodend and this became a Quaker meeting house in the eighteenth century.

However, a mile further west, adjoining a track down to the coastal plain, is to be found the more obvious settlement of Barnacre. The remains of 400 beehive huts are scattered around, some of which were granaries. Much later, the Romans are known to have occupied this site. They chose it for protection at a time when their power was on the wane.

Cross the moraine at the rather marshy western edge of Devoke Water where it has been breached by Linbeck Gill. Aim for the rising ground at the far side, soon crossing the main bridleway that heads down towards the coast and the village of Waberthwaite (of sausage fame!). No reliable path was evident on a recent visit. Keep right on a general southerly bearing over clusters of broken rock to gain the prestigious summit of White Pike.

Eskdale pink granite adorns the summit of Rough Crag

Spot the Isle of Man and Sellafield from White Pike

The view west over the placid stretch of the Irish Sea reveals a unique aspect; the Isle of Man hills in the distance to the left of the fell's noble obelisk and Sellafield power plant to the right. A study in contrasts to be sure!

From here cast your eye to the south east and a duo of finely honed rocky tops. A thin path points the way to Yoadcastle, making a beeline across the grassy depression between. Surrounded by tiers of naked rock, a stiff scramble is required to stand on this splendid summit. To the north can be seen our next objective, a mere quarter of a mile (402 m) across an easy tract. Only slightly lower in altitude than Yoadcastle, Woodend Height looks down on Devoke Water from its lofty perch, where the boathouse can be picked out at the right edge.

Make a direct descent of the gently shelving grassy northern slopes, aiming for this distinctive landmark.

> *The boathouse was originally built for the occupants of Muncaster Castle as a place of relaxation to fish the waters of the lake. Tramps crossing the moors often took advantage of this welcome shelter, breaking in and using the iron fireplace for warmth and a hot meal.*

If energy still courses through your body after this lonely trek, glance over to the rock-girt fell on your right. Find a chink to breach the fractured armour of Seat How and stand proudly atop this jaunty perch. This final conquest is well worth the effort. Thereafter pick a careful trail down the western flank to rejoin the lake path and so back to the fell road.

Pass the fishing lodge beside Devoke Water

Never a 'Boaring' Moment!

An airy stroll amidst clouds that enhance the view

DISTANCE:	7.5 miles (12.1 km)
HEIGHT:	1500 feet (457 m)
SUMMIT VISITED:	Wild Boar Fell: 2324 feet (708 m)
START/FINISH:	Heading north east from Sedbergh, turn right off the A683 half a mile (800 m) beyond Studfold and park on the old road along the grass verge
GRID REFERENCE:	734007
TERRAIN:	Extensive limestone outcrops surrender to rough moorland with a gritstone capping
NEAREST SHOPS:	Kirkby Stephen
USEFUL MAP:	OS Explorer OL19 Howgill Fells & Upper Eden

Prelude

Although not the most exciting way to ascend Wild Boar Fell, this route is most definitely the least known. In consequence, you will have it to yourself, apart, that is, from the black fell ponies that wander this bleak and lonely wilderness. These western slopes hover above a valley not defined by any watercourse other than the diminuitive Sally Beck.

The commanding presence of Wild Boar Fell is best admired from Mallerstang where the jutting prow of The Nab can be seen in all its glory. Only when we have reached this northerly edge of this walk can the exciting ramparts can be experienced. The upper valley to the west enjoys its own brand of euphoria in the form of the Clouds, thick swathes of light grey stones that line the western flank immediately above where our walk begins.

The Walk

Stroll up the main road for 300 yards (274 m), forking right along a rough track past Street Farm. It is hard to imagine but this was at one time part of the main road linking Sedbergh and Kirkby Stephen. Known as The Street, the name has been handed down to this and the next farm that comprise a tiny hamlet. Ambling along this pastoral sector evokes a gentle period when the pace of life was much more sedate.

After merging with the paved access road, you will pass an unusual crenellated feature on the right. A little further along, watch for another lane breaking right. This soon becomes a rough walled track that passes through a gate before blending into the open fell above. When the wall on your left veers away left down to High Stennerskeugh, stick with the clear track that heads across the gently shelving moorland.

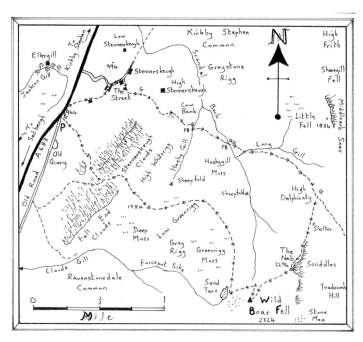

197

A fine shelter for lunch on Wild Boar Fell

After passing a cluster of abandoned stones – once a farm tip – a series of zigzags enable Hashy Gill to be crossed by a newly laid slabbed section. Continue heading in a south-easterly direction to reach a footbridge over Long Gill. Go through two gates, after which the track winds steadily uphill beside Long Gill on the left before leaning right up to the wall-gate on the edge at High Dolphinsty.

From here the magnificent panorama across the Mallerstang Valley can be fully appreciated. The edge is clearly defined, dropping steeply down its eastern face into the valley below. A thin path makes a direct ascent, passing a rough stone shelter on the left. The gnarled gritstone outcropping of The Nab is clearly in view all the way.

Once attained, you can stand atop the wild boar's 'head' to survey his ancestral domain. Here it is said that the final stand was made. As the name implies, these ferocious beasts struck fear into the hearts of simple Dales folk in medieval England. After being hunted down, their tusks were prized as symbols of the triumph of light over darkness. Legend suggests that as the boar population fell into decline, the last in line sought shelter on these bleak and windswept fells of the Upper Eden.

The Stone Men provide a guard of honour for Mallerstang

A poet of the day claimed that a certain Philip Hartley chased the boar onto the plateau, whereupon the cornered beast turned to protect itself. Both the hunter and his dogs were slain, after which a giant pursued the boar onto the summit. A poem was penned to celebrate the event:

> *The Giant with one stroke on loins,*
> *Deprived the boar of life,*
> *Which gave a title to the hill,*
> *That ne'er will pass away,*
> *For it is called Wild Boar Fell,*
> *E'en to this present day.*

In fact a certain Richard de Musgrave is credited with the slaying of the last boar in 1409. His renovated tomb in Kirkby Stephen church revealed a pair of large tusks back in 1847, adding further credence to the story. In more recent times, shepherds indulged in horseracing across this broad expanse.

After pondering over these curious events while standing on The Nab, make your way across the level sward to the actual summit of Wild Boar Fell where a trig column has been planted within a fine eliptical shelter. Observe the stone men standing on the edge of the escarpment half a mile (800 m) to the south.

From the summit make a tentative descent of the rough western slope by aiming initially right from a prominent cairn nearby to avoid stony ground. After dropping down, circle around to the left to reach the delectable hidden gem of Sand Tarn. From here, head north down gentle grass slopes, keeping right of Greenrigg Moss.

Upon reaching the edge of Low Greenrigg, bear left towards a prominent cairn erected on the plateau. Keep to the higher ground to avoid a section of marshland. A thin path becoming steadily stronger follows a meandering course down through a gap in the twin cloud formations of Fell End and Stennerskeugh. This fine descent gives the impression of descending to valley level by parachute, a truly novel experience as you drift down to the old valley road. Enjoy it to the full.

Extraordinary protection for defenders of The Street

A Clash of Arms
Tread the field of battle where King Dunmail raised the Cumbrian flag

DISTANCE:	4.5 miles (7.2 km)
SUMMIT VISITED:	Seat Sandal 2415 feet (736 m)
HEIGHT:	1800 feet (549 m)
START/FINISH:	Use the lay-by adjacent to the climbing hut just before the summit of Dunmail Raise
GRID REFERENCE:	329112
TERRAIN:	Rough fell country with some steep sections and a delightful tarn
NEAREST SHOPS:	Grasmere
USEFUL MAP	OS Explorer OL5 English Lakes north east

Prelude

Dunmail Raise is the lowest of the road passes and has been straightened to accommodate the rapid transit of modern traffic flows. You can, however, still make out the course of the original road veering away across Cotra Breast. In a famous book describing his journey around the Lakes in 1805, William Wordsworth observed that it 'mounts, as you see, in mazes serpentine'.

Few of the passing motorists will have the least notion that they are travelling over the site of the last great battle fought within the vastness of Cumbria. Here occurred the final ignominious defeat of King Dunmail by the Saxon hoards in 945AD. It is claimed that before the conflict, each of the combatants placed a stone on the Dun, the victors retrieving one at the end.

After the battle, Dunmail's body was interred by faithful soldiers beneath the pile of stones that marks the head of the pass. To prevent his mystical crown from falling into the hands of their enemies, the warriors ascended Raise Beck and cast it into Grisedale Tarn before fleeing eastward.

Legend purports that he who wears the enchanted crown has the right to once again rule over the Kingdom of Cumbria. And so each year, the followers of Dunmail retrieve the crown from the murky depths and thence descend to the stone monument there to bestir the entombed spirit beneath. Thus far, the muted cry has risen from the grave, 'Not yet, not yet, the time has not yet come. Wait awhile.' Whereupon the crown is returned to its mythical resting place until the time is right.

The Walk

The legend of Dunmail is something to consider after mounting the ladder-stile to walk across the site of this ancient battleground. A narrow path heads towards the deep gash from which Raise Beck pours forth. Slant over towards the entrance through a sea of bracken. A clear path points the way up the right side of the ravine.

It is a rough ascent but poses no difficulties. Once the gradient eases as the hollow occupied by Grisedale Tarn is neared watch for a path veering right up the grassy bank of Seat Sandal. This is a shortcut that leads directly to the summit. It is only recommended if you suddenly remember it is your wedding anniversary! Otherwise continue ahead into the breathtaking amphitheatre where Dunmail's followers deposited his crown.

Initially rather marshy, another shortcut now presents itself. This skirts the tarn immediately below the crags of Seat Sandal to reach Grisedale Hause. Again, it is only for those in a hurry. Not a trait to be encouraged if the delectable Cumbrian landscape is to be fully savoured. So carry on to the top end of the tarn along a thin trod that joins with the zigzagged route climbing Willie Wife Moor bound for Helvellyn.

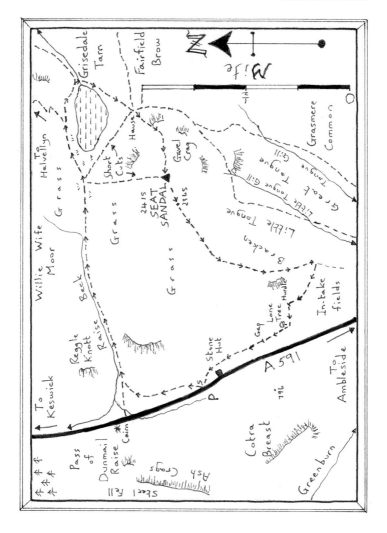

King Dunmail is said to be buried under this cairn

Drop down to cross the beck pouring out of the tarn and join the main track that now climbs back up the far side to reach the wall at Grisedale Hause. From here bear right to mount the acclivitous east ridge of Seat Sandal with Grisedale Tarn nestling serenely in its corrie basin.

The thin path has become much eroded over the years. It now pursues a tortuous route up the craggy elbow parallel to the wall which is crossed as the gradient eases close to a tarn. There then follows a simple stroll to the summit.

This wall is the old boundary line separating Cumberland and Westmorland. It makes an ideal shelter from the keen westerlies that howl their sad lament across the exposed tops. Akin to the baying of

Seat Sandal offers a stunning view over Grasmere Vale

a thousand hounds from hell, the wind whistles and moans through the cracks and crannies.

A certain Miss Attenborough of Ulverston, walking on a fine afternoon, once heard men's voices and a barking dog. On reaching the summit, she found the place empty with not a soul anywhere in sight. A trick of the ether perhaps? Or does Sandulf, the Norse shepherd who gave his name to the fell, still roam this lonely pasture in search of his lost flock?

Our route now lies across a pathless tract heading west-south-west towards a prominent mound 200 yards (183 m) distant. Beyond this a thin track is picked up that descends the left-curving south ridge of

Listen out for ghostly moans on Seat Sandal

Seat Sandal. It is an easy descent with fine views across the Vale of Grasmere. On reaching the intake wall below, bear right making a gradual descent until it begins to rise up the fell.

From here mount a hurdle to drop down, aiming for a large tree below. This section is pathless until the tree is reached from where a thin path heads back towards Dunmail Raise. After passing through a wall-gap, the path improves all the way back to the hut where we rejoin the main road.

A Spy on High

Climb the summit to hear the Cat Bells ring

DISTANCE:	7 miles (11.2 km)
SUMMITS VISITED:	Maiden Moor 1887 feet (575 m), High Spy 2143 feet (653 m)
HEIGHT CLIMBED:	1980 feet (604 m)
START/FINISH:	Go right through Grange and park on a pull-in on the right which has room for six cars. It is located a quarter mile (402 m) before Manesty
GRID REFERENCE:	251182
TERRAIN:	Classical Lakeland scenery of the highest order with an excellent ridge walk above the steep-sided flat valley floor
NEAREST FACILITIES:	Grange-in-Borrowdale
USEFUL MAP:	OS Explorer OL4 English Lakes north west

Prelude

There can be no denying that Borrowdale is justifiably one of the most popular valleys in the Lake District. It is very beautiful, close to Keswick and the major artery of the A66, it is easy to reach from the motorway, all of which means that you cannot expect to have the fells to yourself in high season. Nevertheless, if you set off early, you will certainly miss the crowds, and on the initial stages of this walk, they will invariably be heading for Cat Bells.

Furness Abbey certainly left its mark on Borrowdale, something that is particularly noticeable in the place names. Grange is a hamlet nestling in a cluster of ice-smoothed rocks and was the chief farming settlement occupied by the monks in the thirteenth century. From here a thriving dairy and sheep farming enterprise was begun, which continues to this day, although tourism has now been added as a major source of income in the valley.

Grange lies at the first crossing point of the River Derwent. Here the river splits, which has meant that two connecting stone bridges have had to be built. I know of nowhere else in Cumbria where this anomaly has occurred.

The Walk

Set off by walking up the road to Manesty. Then fork left up a rough track just beyond the old farmhouse. A clear track snakes up the side of Manesty Band. It is a fine ascent and nobody can go astray. It will be even clearer once the renovators have reset the path with the stones that were piled up along the route on my latest visit.

A zigzagged finish over a rocky step brings us to the pass of Hause Gate – a somewhat tuntalogical name, since both 'Hause' and 'Gate' refer to a pass in the hills. Bear left up a less obvious path which experiences a reduced flow of traffic. Climb the ridge until it levels out, at which point branch right off the main path to follow a narrow trod around the steep edge overlooking the Newlands Valley.

Pausing at this point, take time out to admire one of the finest viewpoints north for the pyramid of Cat Bells. The name is thought to be a distortion of Cat Bield, meaning shelter of the wild cat, while nearby Mart Bield offered refuge to the pine marten.

Those who follow the main track that bypasses the summit of Maiden Moor miss out on the fine views from the fell top. There is no doubt that Maiden Moor presents its best side to Newlands. The summit itself is barely worth the effort being a mere handful of stones. Without their guidance, a walker could not hope to establish the precise location. No slackening of pace as we continue along the path to merge with the main track heading for High Spy.

The way ahead is clearly in view as it gradually ascends Narrow Moor towards the defined peak on Blea Crag. A path forks away left to visit

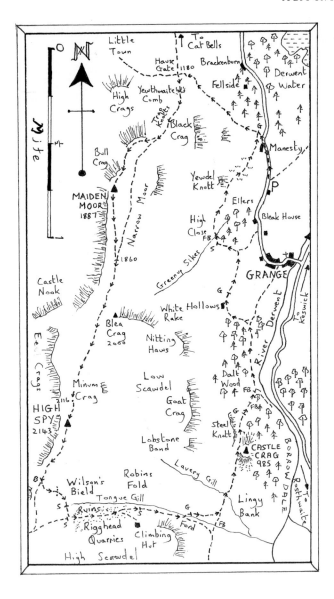

A brutal murderer once stayed at Borrowdale Gates

this rocky excrescence should the detour be desired. Thereafter, an airy walk along the crest of the broad ridge follows. After descending a shallow depression, the path heads straight for the substantial cairn adorning High Spy. We have now exceeded the 2000-foot contour and are in mountain terrain.

Head down the south ridge, aiming towards the depression containing Dalehead Tarn. After half a mile (800 m), lean away to the left along a thin path close to a small tarn. This heads downhill crossing a broken wall known as Wilson's Bield. A short distance further and a fence-stile is mounted, soon joining the main track crossing Rigg Head.

Head left down a steepening gradient that needs care due to its stony nature as it picks a winding course through Rigghead Quarries. Abandoned huts and quarry detritus are all around although the path remains clear. Ignore a fork branching right as you continue down into the valley closing with Tongue Gill. Straddling a fence-stile the path sticks close to the gill. Some 150 yards (137 m) further down, watch for a ford that needs to be crossed to reach the path on the far side.

Go through a gate accompanying a well-graded track that bends left descending in easy stages to merge with the valley route. Head left towards the rising cone of Castle Crag. Those who still have sufficient energy left might be tempted to add this magnificent ancient stronghold to their tally of summits. From the airy perch it is easy to see how a handful of defenders could have controlled access to Upper Borrowdale. Its attainment is a stiff haul and should not be underestimated.

The track descends between steeply enclosed slopes to enter Low Hows Wood through a gate. Cross Broadslack Gill by a footbridge at the bottom, heading north along the gentle flow of the River Derwent.

Somewhere in the sylvan enclave is Kidham Dub, although I have never been able to positively identify the site.

In 1928, a local farmer taking his dog for a walk raised the alarm after discovering the body of a dead Chinese woman close by the secluded pool or 'dub'. Although death was subsequently shown to have been by strangulation, the lady had been severely battered around the head. So what dire circumstances led to such a dastardly crime being perpetrated beneath the leafy boughs of Derwent Water?

It transpired that the two Chinese visitors were newly weds recently arrived on honeymoon from America. Booking into the Borrowdale Gates Hotel north of Grange, they went for a walk in the woods nearby. Chung Yi Miao returned to the hotel alone, claiming that his wife had taken the bus into Keswick to do some shopping.

Having failed to return by the time of the last bus, the hotel owner became alarmed for her safety and informed the local police. They soon arrived and after duly investigating the matter immediately arrested Chung for the murder of his wife.

Throughout his trial, the supposedly distraught husband proclaimed his innocence, counsel for the defence being astutely able to explain away any damning evidence brought against him. But all to no avail, Chung Yi Miao was found guilty of murder and sentenced to death. It later transpired that his wife was unable to participate in connubial relations, a restriction that must have severely overtaxed the new groom's patience on his honeymoon.

Is this the Spy on High?

A last-minute confession prior to his execution revealed his dilemma. Not being able to have a son would bring shame on his family and the ignominy was more than he could bear. Such was the notoriety of the case that it was even reported in the Police Federation's own journal, receiving a front page illustrated spread. No real facts were ever presented to conclusively prove Chung's guilt, however the evidence being circumstantial.

But the devious nature of the rascally upstart can be shown when he was challenged as to why he had hidden his wife's jewellery in his room. He claimed that two sinister Chinese men had been following the pair during their brief sojourn in England and Chung feared he and his wife would be robbed. Yet no mysterious strangers were ever reported in and around the Grange locality at the time.

All is now at peace in the infamous wooded glade where blood was spilt during an uncontrolled frenzy. Think well on this grisly mystery as you continue along the track, watching for a track veering away left to pass through Hollows Farmyard.

The path continues beyond where we go through a gate. Before it enters the wooded enclave of High Close, bear left up a grass bank to a stile at the upper end of the trees. Mount it and slant right to cross a footbridge soon after. The path then heads north skirting the lower slopes of Maiden Moor. Rejoin our outward route just beyond Manesty, heading right back towards Grange.

Manesty is overshadowed by Maiden Moor

Mardale's Hidden Face

Spirits of the dead linger amidst a gargantuan rock garden

DISTANCE:	7.5 miles (12.1 km)
HEIGHT CLIMBED:	1850 feet (564 m)
SUMMITS VISITED:	Branstree: 2333 feet (711 m), Selside Pike: 2142 feet (653 m), Hare Shaw: 1638 feet (499 m)
START/FINISH:	A free car park at the end of Haweswater
GRID REFERENCE:	470108
TERRAIN:	Classic glacial scenery of the highest quality
NEAREST SHOPS:	Shap
USEFUL MAP:	OS Explorer OL5 English Lakes north east

Prelude

No finer dale head can be experienced anywhere else in Lakeland than that surrounding the feeder streams of Haweswater, the reservoirs supply Manchester with its water. Nothing can overcome the sense of grandeur and majesty that permeates the ether as one approaches the road end at Mardale Head. Truly this is a land fashioned by giants with fell wanderers in mind.

For those who relish the feel of hard rock under their boots, this craggy fastness offers a veritable cornucopia to set the pulse racing and the heart pounding in anticipation. Laid out in perfect harmony, nature's treasure strove provides a wild and romantic setting in which to engage in a walk of breath taking intensity.

213

On the final approach to the head of the valley on the right of the wooded promontory known as The Rigg lies the site of Mardale Green. Drowned to accommodate an insatiable urban appetite for water, the village was dismantled in 1935 when the permanent residents of the graveyard were exhumed to be re-interred in Shap cemetery.

A further six years were to pass, however, before the area of water in the valley was effectively trebled and Mardale Green sank into the pages of history. Except during rare periods of drought when the ancient bones of the old settlement are resurrected, visitations are now confined to those bound for the heights above the clouds.

Tracks forking off in all directions were once used by packhorses travelling between the valleys of Lakeland. Today, these hallowed portals have been infiltrated by modern-day adventurers seeking to escape the pressures of a hectic society.

The Walk

Leave the road through a gate, bearing left to ascend the clear track aiming for Gatescarth Pass. This is a steady climb up to the fence marking the head of the pass, beyond which the track drops down into Longsleddale. Head left here following a thin path on the left side of the fence all the way up onto the summit of Branstree.

The highest point is left of a wall-corner marked by a small cairn. A circular stone triangulation marker is an unusual feature of the summit, replacing the traditional column. However, a much better place to stop is at the fine cairn erected on Artlecrag Pike. Standing proudly visible 200 yards (183 m) to the north east amidst a rash of stones, it offers a handy backrest to linger awhile and enjoy the stunning view across Mardale.

From here, continue heading north east down a clear path to rejoin the ridge fence. Accompanying this up a gentle grade will bring you onto Selside Pike where a robust cairn has been erected. From here, head down the gently shelving broad grassy ridge, still maintaining a north-easterly direction. Take note of the old corpse road below along

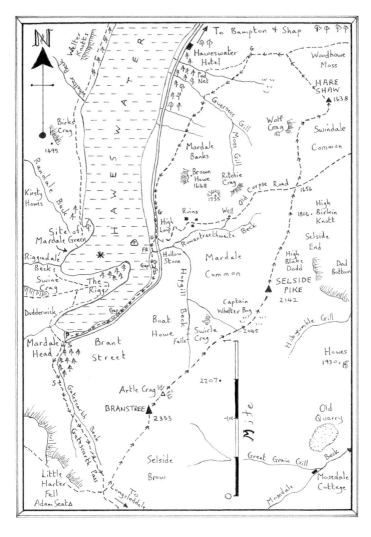

Old Mardale Green lies in this cove beneath Haweswater

which the coffins passed from Mardale down into Swindale then onward to Shap.

One story involves a murderer whose heinous crime went undetected during his lifetime. The felon clearly went to his maker with a guilty conscience as the heavens erupted in tempestuous fury whilst his body was in transit along the corpse road. Beset with terror, the horse bolted with the laden coffin strapped to its back.

When it finally re-appeared some three months later, the coffin was still firmly secured in place. By this time the blackguard's skulduggery had come to light and some say this was a belated punishment enacted by the victim's spirit.

216

An unusual triangulation marker on Branstree

Our route forks away left from the main ridge to cross the Old Road heading due north towards the outcropping of Wolf Crag. Keep right of this rocky knott aiming for the rising ground ahead which is Hare Shaw. Surmounted by a modest cairn, this is the highest point along these indeterminate uplands to the east of Haweswater.

From here strike down a knobbly slope heading north west to reach a corner of the wall enclosing the Naddle Valley. Bear left along this to crest a low rise until a cross-wall is reached. Go through the gate veering sharp left. Do not be tempted by the clear track on the right which quickly loses height. (On my first visit, I followed this and had to retrace my steps to regain the upper path where it crossed the beck of Pod Net.) The main path thereafter descends at a gradual pace to cross the wooded ravine of Guerness Gill. Beyond this cutting it rises over Aaron Bield before continuing downhill towards the valley road below.

Paralleling the road for 200 yards, the path terminates at a gate where you then join the road for a stroll down to where the Corpse Road crosses. Hang a right through a gate to drop down to the waters below. Then head left along the lakeside path back to Mardale Head. This is a splendid walk for the busy season when you are more than likely to have these eastern fells to yourself.

Artlecrag Pike offers a more impressive display